LANDSCAPES,
LAWNS & LIES:

LANDSCAPES, LAWNS & LIES:

How to Avoid Shady Practices That Cost You Time, Money and More

JOHN WRIGHT JR. AND SONDRA J. WRIGHT

*Bella*HOUSE PUBLISHING
Greensboro, North Carolina

LANDSCAPES, LAWNS & LIES:

How to Avoid Shady Practices That
Cost You Time, Money and More

ISBN 978-0-9831265-7-7
Library of Congress Control Number: 2016930228

Manufactured in the United States of America

BellaHOUSE PUBLISHING

BellaHouse Publishing
P. O. Box 36355
Greensboro, NC 27416-6355
www.bellahousepub.com

Website:
www.jwwright.com

Cover art by Sean Allum
Interior illustrations by V. Shane
Cover and interior design by Juanita Dix • www.designjd.net

TABLE OF CONTENTS

DEDICATION

To the loving memory of my late father,
John W. Wright, Sr.,
the most honorable man with the
greenest thumb I have ever known.
It is my joy to take a *page from your book,*
and with thoughtful regard, preface the
ideas I will share inside these pages
with your sage expression…

"This is just me talking."

INTRODUCTION

"All that is necessary for the triumph of evil is that good men do nothing." —Edmund Burke

In a perfect world, whenever you entered into an agreement with an individual or a business to exchange goods or services for some monetary consideration, you would customarily and enthusiastically get exactly what you pay for. Those you hire would possess the requisite levels of knowledge, skill, experience, and professionalism to fix your issue correctly or implement your vision accurately and with a high level of expertise. Not only that, tradespeople would be passionate about their craft, and contractors would show up on time, sufficiently manned with a well-trained staff who have been aptly supplied with the appropriate tools and equipment for the task before them. And to round out this utopian vision, these tradespeople and contractors would work efficiently, manage the budget wisely, treat your property with the same care and respect with which they would treat their own, clean up thoroughly before they leave, and not cause any careless or unnecessary damage to your home or property.

However, in this not-so-perfect world we live in, perhaps the very best you could ever hope for is someone like me; an honest, conscientious individual who is tired of seeing good, hardworking, unsuspecting consumers get had, hoodwinked, took, bamboozled, run amuck and led astray, and sincerely desires to do something to help level the playing field.

Before I begin my journey of saving the world from duplicitous characters, let me at least introduce myself. My name is John Wright, Jr., a licensed landscape contractor, master gardener, and certified paver installer with a degree in landscape architecture. Since being certified as a landscape contractor for more than three decades, I have served my community and communities throughout the state of North Carolina proudly and with integrity by designing and installing quality landscapes and hardscapes, and performing grounds maintenance and management for homeowners, commercial property owners and property managers, alike.

In essence, I have spent my entire thirty years plus professional career in the landscape industry. Over the course of this long and satisfying career, I have enjoyed the great fortune of being able to continually hone my craft and grow my level of industry knowledge, skill, and expertise through a wide and varied range of professional experiences. I worked for others, owned my own company, collaborated with seasoned professionals, and mentored more than a few newcomers in the startup of their own businesses. I am also privileged to have worked with a diverse array of individuals as well as both public and private sector firms.

It goes without saying that I have considerable respect for the industry, those who love it like I do, the clients and customers we serve, and the generation of young green industry professionals coming up behind us who are poised and ready to take the wheel. Unfortunately, as with all industries, an element of mischief and malfeasance exists among those claiming the title of landscape professional that must be addressed and exposed.

Regrettably, over the course of my career, I witnessed many examples of dishonest, unethical behavior and understand firsthand the damaging effects it can have on people, property, and even relationships. The crooked business tactics I refer to include but are not limited to the following examples:

- Intentional misrepresentation and deception
- Bait and switch project materials
- Refusal to honor warranties
- Denial of personal responsibility or accountability
- Harassment, intimidation or bullying
- Disparagement of the property owner's truthfulness, integrity and character
- Illegal use of threats (mechanics lien, contacting employer, court judgments, etc.) to get payment

When consumers realize that they are victims of fraudulent contractor activity and/or unethical business practices, the impact can potentially be devastating in countless and varied ways. In addition to the obvious potential economic losses, very often consumers may also pay steep psychological and emotional costs.

It starts the very moment a consumer suddenly finds him/herself unable to reach the contractor or their calls to the contractor to complete a project or fix faulty work go ignored or unreturned. When the gradual, sullen realization sets in that one may have just overpaid, been conned, or should have gotten a written agreement and neglected to do so, or one is faced with the very real threat of being sued or having a lien placed on her or his home or property, overwhelming and crushing feelings of betrayal and helplessness are typically not far behind. In turn, this may lead to nagging guilt, shame, self-blame, and self-doubt, or blaming a spouse or significant other; exacting a severe emotional toll on both individuals and relationships.

Unfortunately, chances are many of you reading this are nodding your head in recognition and agreement at this very moment. You can relate to what I am saying because many of you had or know someone personally who had one or more similar experiences. If so, touch your neighbor, and say, "Neighbor..." Never mind. I digressed. Take a second, seriously, and remember how you felt. What did you have to go through to resolve the issue, or was it ever really resolved? What consequences did you face? What effects did the experience have on you, your spouse or significant other, your family, or your relationship?

To make an already bad situation worse, in many instances, due largely to the lack of consumer complaints against them, the disdainful, unscrupulous individuals perpetrating and perpetuating these deceitful, unscrupulous actions simply move from project to project. They never correct or even attempt to correct a problem, but are content to repeatedly inflict the same economic, emotional, and psychological damage on other good, hardworking, unsuspecting consumers.

There are several reasons customers allow this cycle of fraudulent deception to play itself out, again and again. Curiously, the reluctance of consumers to even admit they have been had often prevents them from reporting the incident to the proper agency or authority. Perhaps the wronged consumer does not know what agency or organization to report the incident to or the appropriate steps he or she must take to be made whole.

If you found yourself in this situation today, do you know how to go about reporting the problem? Do you know what steps to take to possibly recover any losses you sustained? Do you know which agencies or offices to contact?

Another primary reason these incidents go unreported is that all too often, indications that a contractor engaged in any deception or wrongdoing are not always readily apparent to a consumer. Some really bad actors are very adept at covering up their malfeasance. Take for example, this actual scenario.

A consumer arrives home and is greeted by a very excited, animated neighbor who says: "You will never believe what happened here today!" The neighbor goes on to explain, "Your lawn company came by earlier. They didn't see me watching from the window but this guy jumped out of the truck, sprayed a line of fertilizer down the length of your driveway, sprayed another line of fertilizer beside the length your walkway, and then hopped back in the truck and left! Off to the next unsuspecting sucker I guess. I couldn't believe it! There is no way he was here for more than about five minutes or so. Hey, if you're giving your money away like that, let me throw my hat in the ring! I'm more than happy to do nothing for it."

Now, let me see if I can paint you a clear picture of what just occurred here. The homeowner paid the lawn service to fertilize the entire lawn – front, back and side. However, instead of doing the entire lawn as the homeowner contracted and paid for, the lawn service's representative sprayed fertilizer only along the strips of lawn that ran alongside the driveway and the sidewalk. Why these two areas specifically?

The answer is simple. The company's representative knew the edge of the concrete sidewalk and driveway would retain some evidence of the spraying in the form of the fertilizer residue. The presence of this residue is meant to deceive the homeowner into believing that the lawn service actually visited on that day and fertilized the entire lawn as agreed, and to the satisfaction of the homeowner. However, the unsuspecting homeowner only received a small fraction of the service that he or she paid for and would have been none the wiser had his or her neighbor not been there to witness it. Sometimes having a nosy, "ahem," concerned neighbor is decidedly a good thing.

As you can see from the above scenario, dishonest, unethical contractors expend a great deal of time and energy devising all manner of deceptive schemes and shortcuts intended to insure that consumers do not have a clue they are being deceived. However, even if wrongdoing is detected, as explained previously, there are a number of reasons a consumer still may not complain. Perhaps you had the unfortunate incident of one of the following experiences:

- You get that nagging feeling "something" has happened but not a shred of evidence to support what your instincts are telling you.
- You pointed to yourself or some other condition, but not the contractor, as being all or part of the problem.
- You felt embarrassed, ashamed, or humiliated and are convinced if something is wrong, chances are it was probably your fault.
- After adding up the economic and/or emotional cost of complaining, you decided to just let it go, believing the cost of pursuing any reparative or recuperative actions would exceed any potential benefit.
- Believed any damages you may recoup, or even the chances of actually recovering any damages, were so minimal they do not really compel you to act.

And homeowners are not the only ones vulnerable to being victimized by shady contractors. The problem of fraudulent, misleading or deceptive business practices is a large scale one that happens to many and at many levels including: government entities and agencies at the local, state, and federal levels; both public and private businesses; hospitals; apartment complexes; colleges and universities. No one or thing is immune.

The faith community is particularly vulnerable since church governing bodies usually do not believe that people, in general, would be so audacious as to take advantage of a church. Church leadership can be especially trusting (and forgiving), but most often these governing bodies simply do not have an agent or a representative who possesses the knowledge and insight needed to oversee a project, placing these institutions at the complete mercy of the contractor. I have done a number of pro bono corrective landscape jobs for churches that relied on deacons, trustees, or a committee of other members to serve as liaison between the church and the contractor. Unfortunately, none of these individuals or groups representing the interests of the church proved knowledgeable or insightful enough about the process to recognize and demand the correction of issues when they occurred.

Above all, please know and believe that a contractor is known by his or her work, good and bad. Ethical contractors—whether a single individual, a small business with a few employees, or a major corporation employing thousands—do not exploit customers. They are committed to executing their trade or craft with a high level of skill and expertise and dealing with customers fairly and honestly without fail. Ethical contractors take great pride in their work, and love and see the value in a satisfied customer. Therefore, he or she wants and welcomes the opportunity to respond to and remedy as completely and reasonably as possible any and all instances of customer dissatisfaction.

On the other hand, an unethical contractor cares very little about the quality of their work; he or she is mostly concerned with getting that "check" in their greasy, sweaty little palms and very quickly moving on to the next victim...er...project. So, your dissatisfaction annoys them extensively as, for the most part, you have become purely a nuisance – a bothersome little gnat; an irritant who is simply costing additional time and money. These contractors find it more beneficial to move on to the next unsuspecting customer than invest more time and energy in insuring the satisfaction of the existing customer.

While an ethical contractor will always welcome your call and treat you and your concerns with the utmost respect, a contractor who engages in bad-faith practices will ignore your calls, and may even become verbally abusive should you dare complain or point out any fault in their work. Beware, because these shifty characters can often be very skilled manipulators who excel more at denying, projecting and blame shifting than at the actual trade they represent. If only they would dedicate themselves to mastering some real technique.

Happily, I can sincerely, confidently, completely lacking any guilt or shame say I am of the former category; the ethical contractor. For me, landscaping is a passion, and I take extreme pride in my work and in this industry. I consider myself and others like me to be artisans in every sense of the word. Because of my sincere and deeply held pride in myself and my industry, I feel a tremendous obligation to protect individuals and organizations against what I perceive to be the many corrupt practices and behaviors plaguing the industry. I cannot, of course, force a dishonest business or business owner to become honest, or purge the industry of the unscrupulous behaviors of dishonest contractors. What I can do within the pages of this book is try to equip you with the knowledge you need to spot and avoid unethical practices that could cost you time, money, peace of mind, and so much more.

> *"I cannot teach anybody anything.*
> *I can only make them think."* —Socrates

Throughout these pages, so that you might gain realistic insight into some sketchy industry practices, the woman who I am proud and very much blessed to have as my partner in business and in life, my wife Sondra, will share a few scenarios based on actual events. She will illustrate several points using the fictitious contractor she created called C. D. Guy, so named after his "seedy" business practices. C. D. is the owner of Shadyscapes Lawn and Landscaping, Co., a fictitious commercial and residential landscaping company specializing in "shady" landscape deals.

However, before we proceed, allow me to reiterate that this is a fictional business owner and a hypothetical business we are using for dramatic and demonstrative purposes only. If you are in the industry and happen to be reading this book, let me assure you that any resemblance between yourself and C. D. Guy you feel you might perceive is purely coincidental. However, should you sense any likeness between yourself and our fictional C. D. Guy, remember that when you throw a rock into a crowd of people, the person who yells out is the person you hit. I hope this book will be the catalyst to your reassessing how you do business and making the necessary changes in the right direction.

In addition to looking at contractor practices, we will also explore some of the unnecessary risks property owners take that land them in a jam, or worse, pose a serious threat to themselves and others. From doing business on a handshake to underestimating the complexity of do-it-yourself (DIY) projects, seemingly small actions present major consequences in the world of Landscapes, Lawns & Lies. Fear not, however. To ensure you do not make costly or even harmful errors in judgement, you will find a wealth of tips warning you of what to avoid sprinkled throughout the pages of this book. It is also important to note that because my licensure as landscape contractor and majority of my knowledge of local rules and statutes is applicable exclusively to the state of North Carolina, much of the information in this book will pertain specifically to businesses, residents, and contractors operating within North Carolina. Be sure to check with your own state and local authorities as regulations can vary greatly from state to state.

CHAPTER 1

PAY NOW OR PAY LATER:

Is the Price Really Right?

"If you live by price, you die by price." —Alen Majer

These days we are all watching our dollars a little closer, and we all want to get the most bang for our buck. Many commercial and residential property owners have fallen into the low price trap of opting to choose their landscape professionals based on price alone, believing it to be in the best interest of their bottom line.

Your landscaping project is an investment that should be safeguarded and protected from start to finish, and beyond. Whether looking to install new landscaping or maintain or enhance existing landscaping, it is important that you do your homework to ensure that you are making the very best investment and getting the very best value for your money. You must never base your decision to choose one landscaping company over others solely on price. This decision should be systematically and intelligently thought out, taking into account many different factors.

First, I must urge you to proceed with the utmost caution if you receive an extremely low bid or estimate (particularly one that is substantially lower than the next lowest bid or estimate). As the saying goes, if something seems too good to be true, it usually is. When a bid comes in too low there is usually a hidden cost to be paid, either immediately or in the long run, and you, the consumer, will typically be the one who pays.

To help illustrate this point, allow me to introduce you to our favorite duplicitous landscape character, C. D. Guy, and let us see what manner of mischief we find him engaged in today:

> C. D. Guy does a lot of work that involves land clearing – the removal of stumps, trees, limbs, brush and other vegetation. Whatever C. D. Guy removes from a property owner's property or project site has to be taken somewhere away from the site to be disposed of. Proper and acceptable practice within the landscaping industry is to first make an attempt to dispose of land-clearing waste at a permitted composting, chipping, or mulching facility. What we are not able to recycle, we must dispose of in an approved landfill. However, disposing of land-clearing waste is not free; this costs money. C. D. does not want this additional expense cutting into his profit, so what does he do?

Well, he just might simply bury the waste somewhere on your property. Over time, as the waste decomposes, its mass decreases and the soil on top begins to sink, you begin to notice this ever expanding, ever deepening mysterious dent in your lawn. Or, he might find some remote, seemingly inconspicuous location or an empty, deserted lot and dump the waste there. Later, not only do city or county workers find the pile of waste, but they also find evidence, some old utility bills thrown out with the pile, connecting that waste back to you and your property. The next thing you know, intimidating, scary looking government officials are standing on your doorstep with a citation and a hefty fine, and even though you yourself did not dump the waste and, in fact, were not even aware that the waste had been illegally dumped, because C. D. was working for you, he is considered to be your agent. Therefore, the onus for paying this fine falls on you. While you would love to point the finger at somebody, somewhere, you have no one to blame but yourself. I told you when we began that C. D. is shady, but hey, you wanted to save a few dollars, right? Or so you thought.

Although N.C. General Statute 14-399(e) classifies the illegal dumping of waste for commercial purposes as a Class I Felony, illegal dumping is just one practice a disreputable contractor may take to cut costs. Here are some additional cost cutting practices that will impact you in a more direct way:

- *Using low quality materials* – The quality of materials can definitely matter in the look, durability and longevity of your project. Stay on top of your project so the contractor does not "sell" you on higher quality, more expensive materials but do a bait and switch by using lower quality, less expensive materials in the actual installation.

- *Using smaller size trees, plants, or shrubs than agreed to* – The cost of plant materials can vary greatly based on the size of the plant. Make sure the sizes of all plant materials installed are the sizes you were quoted and are paying for.

- *Using the least expensive project materials available* – Are you having a deck, patio, pergola, walkway, or retaining wall built? Be aware of the practice of a contractor drawing up a quote based on the contractor installing, for example, a $10 per linear foot material, but instead the contractor installs a $3 per linear foot material, and then pockets the $7 per linear foot difference.

- *Deviating from the project's plans, specifications, or agreed upon terms and conditions* – Your project plans, specifications, and agreed upon terms and conditions make up your project roadmap. This roadmap should carefully spell out the particulars, like quantities, material types, whether trees are to be staked or not, whether plants are to be watered, and if so, how much and for how long. Will the contractor construct a proper surface utilizing the required base material before installing your patio pavers? Is your concrete retaining wall constructed with the properly sized units?

Remember, these are all items that should be a part of your estimate and should be included in your contract. Are you knowledgeable enough to determine if your work is being executed properly? Do you have a competent owner's agent or representative acting on your behalf? If not, who is verifying the work and looking out for your best interest? In the absence of the proper and adequate checks and balances, a goldmine of opportunity exists for the unscrupulous contractor to cut quantities, switch materials, and skip steps that dupe you and increase his or her own bottom line.

I recently came across a quote that resonated quite loudly with me. Although I have pondered this very sentiment on many occasions, I have never seen it expressed so clearly. The quote, a reflection of price and risk, is from an article entitled "The Common Law of Business Balance" and is credited to John Ruskin, a leading 19th century British art critic, author, and poet. Ruskin was a creative thinker and influential social critic; and today Ruskin College in Oxford is named for him.

Consider Mr. Ruskin's advice:

"There is hardly anything in the world that someone cannot make a little worse and sell a little cheaper, and the people who consider price alone are that person's lawful prey. It's unwise to pay too much, but it's worse to pay too little. When you pay too much, you lose a little money—that is all. When you pay too little, you sometimes lose everything, because the thing you bought was incapable of doing the thing it was bought to do. The common law of business balance prohibits paying a little and getting a lot — it can't be done. If you deal with the lowest bidder, it is well to add something for the risk you run, and if you do that you will have enough to pay for something better."

As you can imagine, this quote speaks, in the main, to those who consider price to be an exact measure of, and in always direct proportion to, quality. In other words, pay a lot to get a lot. There are many people who operate under the faulty assumption of that which has the highest price tag is inherently of better quality.

Let's use this brief anecdote a friend shared with me as an example:

I have an older family member who prides herself in 'only buying the very best.' She grew up in extreme poverty, and has worked very hard to attain a high degree of success, both professionally and financially, so I agree with her that she indeed deserves to have only the best of everything. However, she is of the mindset that 'the very best' always translates to 'the highest priced.'

Recently, she purchased a new computer. She walked into the store, found the computer with the steepest price tag, and purchased it, thinking that this computer just had to be the cream of the crop; the finest the store had to offer. After all, wasn't it the most expensive?

She called me over to set her computer up for her, and I was somewhat taken aback when I heard what she paid. In fact, I was even rather perturbed thinking that the salesperson had taken complete advantage of her, but she assured me this was not the case; this was the computer she selected. As I read through all the features, functions, and capacity of her new computer, I realized what she had actually paid all that money for was the computer manufacturer's well-known name. In actuality, she could have purchased a computer with practically double the capacity for about 75% of what she paid for the computer she purchased.

I have observed that in equating price with quality, she often spends much more than need be. In fact, in equating price with quality without considering any other factors, much of the time she sadly ends up with a product of even lesser quality.

This is personally not my style. I am not one who believes, and never would try to convince anyone else to believe, that the more you spend, the better quality you can expect. It is just not always true that higher quality costs more. However, in making this point, this classic quote by Ruskin also speaks to the irrationality of the low-price purchasing decision. While on the one hand, spending more does not necessarily guarantee greater quality, on the other hand, going with the lowest price does not necessarily guarantee greater savings. Price is but one piece of the puzzle.

Ruskin's observation completely aligns with my way of thinking. We err in automatically selecting contractors based on the low-price alone. I see the negative results of doing so played out repeatedly in the field. This is a major source of contention for those of us who deliver quality, reliability and trust, but also a very difficult conversation to have without sounding preachy or coming across as trying to advance our own agendas.

Time and time again, property owners fall victim to dubious landscape and lawn care arrangements when depending almost solely on the low price rule in their landscape professional selection process. This transaction generally begins with property owners appearing to have the upper hand in the relentless quest for the best deal. Most of us in the industry have, on more than one occasion, been greeted with a stern, "I'm price shopping, and I'll buy when I get the best price!"

The attitude and belief that the lowest price is the best price and only price worth a property owner's time and consideration are quite prevalent, but in the same instance, they are also quite faulty. Following close behind is the mindset that any contractor whose price is higher than his competitor's price is somehow cheating, attempting to take advantage of, or in some way defraud the property owner. However, nothing could be further from the truth. Anyone can sharpen a pencil, crunch the numbers, and meet or beat the price quoted by a competitor for work he or she claims is identical in scope and in quality. But, as I will demonstrate throughout this book, this is not always true. All quotes are not created equal;

the devil, as the saying goes, is the details. There are many factors to be considered that when left out of the equation, are detrimental to your best interest, the same best interest you were attempting to protect by scouting exclusively for the best price.

Unfortunately, most property owners lack the capacity and experience necessary for making a valid comparison between proposals based on values other than price. In fact, if you are requesting quotes but do not have a set of plans and specifications along with a very clear, reasonable vision of what you actually want, you cannot expect to receive a true "apples-to-apples" comparison. Each contractor or company will submit you a quote based on its interpretation of what it believes you want, what it perceives your vision to be, and as a result, the prices you get back will be ambiguous, at best.

So how do you eliminate the ambiguity and ensure that each contractor price quote you receive is based on a homogenous set of requirements? One way would be a comprehensive scope of work, which would identify what the contractors general responsibilities are, what paperwork or proofs the contractor would be required to provide, what services the contractor will perform, and how specifically the contractor will carry out the work. Clearly spelling out all that is expected and required allows each bidder an opportunity to take the exact same elements into consideration when preparing their quote. Remember, even the best, most capable contractors cannot read your mind. Providing the contractor with as much information as possible is crucial to obtaining complete and accurate professional bids and quotations.

All men are created equal. All landscapers are not.

The average person looks at a landscape estimate and wonders what about this contractor makes him or her so special that they can justify this price. The average person thinks, "Really?! What is one landscaper going to do, that the other landscaper can't do? All we're talking about is dropping some trees and flowers in the dirt! Anyone can do that!" But this is a mindset and belief that has backfired on businesses and homeowners alike, simply because the average person does not understand what a talented and proven landscape professional brings to the table.

Many a landscape contractor, including myself, has sat down with a potential client, discussed their project in detail, and gathered all the information necessary to prepare a design and proposal. Once prepared, we have then scheduled a follow-up meeting to review the plan and proposal, answer any questions, and address any concerns. So far, so good, right? At the end of this meeting, the inquiring potential client thanks you for your time and politely explains that he or she is waiting for another estimate to come in, or perhaps just needs some additional time to consider your proposal.

A couple of weeks pass, so you place a friendly call just to follow-up. However, you cannot help but notice the difference in the tone and energy of the conversation, and the potential client makes an excuse to quickly rush you off the phone. A gut feeling tells you to take a quick detour past their property on the way to your next appointment, and when you do, your suspicions are confirmed—your design, your concept, and your ideas have been implemented at their property, by someone other than you.

If landscape plagiarism was an actual concept, this would perfectly define and demonstrate it! It seems the homeowner perhaps had someone else in mind to do the installation all along. Maybe he or she was not trained or equipped to do the design, or lacked access to sources for some of the materials required for the project. In all likelihood, they are not even a qualified or experienced landscape professional. Maybe it was Joe Blow who did an outstanding power wash for the neighbor three houses down, or the college student who works part-time in the paint department at the neighborhood hardware, lawn and garden center. Who knows? At any rate, you are not the tiniest bit pleased with what you see.

The homeowner used you, your time, and, perhaps most importantly, your expertise to provide their chosen installer with all the details and information they felt would be needed to complete the project. Yet, just as you are about to drive away with important lessons learned and a few mental notes about what you will do differently next time, a few problems leap out at you like deer on a country road. It is not as if you are really trying to be critical of another installer's work, but there are, in fact, some noticeable concerns.

Some of the plants are not spaced properly and lack sufficient room for the sunlight and airflow necessary for their development. The two accent trees, planted at either corner of the house, are planted much too close to the house. While attractive today, when these trees mature, not only can they cause significant damage to the roof and gutters, but the root system can damage the home's foundation as well.

In addition, a couple of expensive ornamental trees are planted too deeply. This is one of the surefire, quickest ways to kill a tree because oxygen cannot get to its root system, causing the tree to literally choke to death. Next, you notice deep tire tracks that have destroyed a significant portion of the recently installed sod, probably when the mulch was being delivered and dropped. Oops! You sure hope someone is going to fix that!

Many contractors have learned the hard way, unfortunately, to also protect themselves from unethical consumer behaviors. While thankfully this scenario is not indicative of the majority of good, honest, hardworking property owners I encounter, it has and does happen frequently enough that those in the industry have learned to be a little more careful with our intellectual property. Through the process of trial and error, we have learned to recognize the warning signs of a customer or homeowner seeking to either take advantage of our knowledge and expertise or discover a loophole to get out of paying.

You know perhaps as well as I, that people will often go to extreme measures to save a few shekels. My wife, for example, will scour the Internet in relentless pursuit of a percent-off coupon, Groupon, or LivingSocial deal before she commits to purchasing anything. She just needs the satisfaction of knowing she is not paying a penny more than the next customer. And I get that. Honestly, I do. There is indeed some satisfaction in a "great deal." Wasting money however, is never a good deal. In this case, the cost of a project done incorrectly, plus the added expense of undoing the mistakes and redoing it properly, is an unfortunate waste.

You cannot underestimate the added value of hiring a trained, experienced landscape professional. A trained, experienced landscape professional brings to the table a defined and proven skill set and a certain degree of competence, supported by a keen understanding and a high level of expertise. Furthermore, he or she comes to the table after having invested a significant amount of time in training, completing both the necessary education, as well as time in the field, mastering his or her craft. This professional sits at the table with confidence because they have made a monetary investment in the proper, highest quality (not to be confused with the most expensive) tools and equipment and hired and trained a team of skilled, competent and passionate employees.

Finally, you as the consumer can be confident in your decision to trust this person with your vision because a high degree of professionalism is evident in their willingness to undergo the process of obtaining the proper licensure and credentials and then seek and gain membership to the relevant professional associations. Should anything go awry, the steps to protect the both of you have been taken through the acquisition and maintenance of the required types and sufficient levels of liability insurance.

All of these assets are tremendously valuable. Their worth, unfortunately, is not often understood or appreciated until an unfortunate incident forces you to realize that hindsight is indeed 20/20. It is a tragic phenomenon, this post event realization that grabs ahold only when you are facing a real maelstrom. Often only in retrospect does the light bulb finally come on, the vision becomes a lot clearer, and the reality that there were many other values worthy of your consideration sets in.

While writing this section, my wife reminded me of a particular experience that I have asked her to share with you:

When John and I first started in business together, it was always somewhat disappointing for me after putting so much time and care into pricing a project only to have our price rejected and the customer select someone else for their project. I guess John did not enjoy it much himself, but he was always so calm and cool about it. Whenever someone thought our price was too high, I immediately wanted to respond with a percent off, a coupon code, a price match—whatever it took to get the business; but not John.

He would always say to me, "We've given them a fair price to do the job right. They can pay us now, or they can pay us later." Of course, I would scoff to myself and think, "Pay us later? They're not going to pay us at all, babe. They're not our customer!" How in the world could he be so calm when we had just lost money?

But when it came to pricing a project, he always stuck to his guns. He knew we were knowledgeable and effective and always delivered a quality product, just as we had promised, and at a fair price. As I began to look around and take note of the business practices of some of our competition—showing up late or not showing up at all, disappearing after partially completing a project or sticking the homeowner with shoddy work, and not honoring warranties or, in many cases, not providing a warranty at all—I too became at ease and confident in our first price, fair price approach.

I actually remember a specific instance when I got to see John's *pay us now or pay us later* philosophy at work that will always stand out in my mind. We were working with a married couple who recently made a significant investment in a home and had been referred to us by one of our really good clients. The home they purchased was a slightly older home; however, I could readily see their justifications for doing so in the beauty of the grounds and the wealth of potential this home possessed. And among the many great ideas these very creative new homeowners had for the house was the aesthetic vision to install a nice stone patio to enhance the back of the property.

We met several times in an effort to get a real feel for the couple, their tastes, and their plans for the space and gather enough information so that we might develop a clear picture of their vision; what they actually wanted. We constructed a mockup that brought a lot of character to the space, and one we believed demonstrated an exquisite marriage of our design interpretations with their personal style, needs and requirements. In addition, we furnished them with samples of material selections that really gave life to their vision by incorporating interesting and unique colors, textures, lines and shapes.

After all was said and done, we were more than confident that we exceeded their expectations and captured their vision perfectly. We came highly recommended to this couple, we partnered with and walked with them through this process, so naturally when we presented them with the proposal, the price to bring the vision to life, their hesitation to move forward caught us completely by surprise.

They ultimately decided our estimate was too high, which left me somewhat dismayed. Not only did I feel we had developed a great rapport with this couple, but we had developed a tremendous amount of respect for them as well, and sincerely believed that the respect was mutual. I would have bet the entire farm, all of the equipment and every piece of livestock that we would be the contractor implementing this incredible plan. In fact, I had never even considered that they might balk at our estimate, which, if I may say so myself, was a really great price.

I immediately went into a tizzy! I wanted to meet, find out the amount of their lowest quote, take another ten percent off that, and sign the contract! I just could not bear the thought of so much effort not producing anything so yes, at that time, I believed it much better to lower the price and make something than lose them as clients and walk away with nothing. Plus, I knew we were the right contractor for the job! Not only did we have the appropriate expertise for the project, but we were genuinely interested in their goals for this project and helping them achieve the absolute best outcome. However, true to form my solid as a rock husband held my hand, looked me in the eye and said rather matter-of-factly, "It's okay, sweetheart. They can pay us now, or they can pay us later."

Well, I was more than a bit incredulous. It was not as though "pay us later" happened on every job we did not land, and when it did, it was usually after something had gone terribly wrong. But this – this was a sharp, smart, professional couple, and I had every confidence in their ability to handle their business, so I just needed to put my big girl panties on, accept this temporary disappointment as just one of the costs of being in business, and move on graciously. When the sun came up the next day that is exactly what I did.

Well nevertheless, and very much to my surprise, approximately fifteen months later, "later" did indeed arrive. My mouth dropped wide open when John told me the husband had contacted him, explained that there were some issues with the patio, and asked if we would please come take a look and advise them on the direction they should take. He did not give a lot of detail over the phone, so we headed to their home not fully knowing what to expect.

When installed correctly, stone pavers can be a stunning addition to a home's outdoor space. While the beauty of natural stone is its greatest appeal, property owners enjoy a number of additional benefits such as durability, low maintenance and excellent safety against slip and falls – making it a popular choice for pools, patios and walkways. When done incorrectly, however, stone pavers are an absolute nightmare. Not only are these incorrectly installed pavers horrible to look at, but when they begin to shift what they leave in their wake are annoyingly uneven surfaces, so outdoor furniture frustratingly, irritatingly, and uncomfortably rocks. Even worse, the danger of injury by someone actually tripping and falling on this jagged terrain presents a real risk to those living in the home as well as visiting neighbors, relatives and friends; exposing the homeowner to financial liability.

Unfortunately, we arrived only to discover both the patio and the marriage pretty much the same shape—a little rough, a little rocky and a little ragged. Their patio was in really bad shape because it was installed incorrectly. John removed a section of the pavers and discovered that the contractor installed them on top of a bed of sand but had neglected to use any base material underneath—a common mistake made by inexperienced installers and a common cost-cutting measure taken by unethical installers. However, to ensure proper drainage, stability, and a level surface on which to set the stones, this crucial step cannot be omitted when installing pavers. Without a proper base, the pavers will invariably begin to sink and shift, resulting in the very problems now plaguing these frustrated homeowners.

The wife was weary and had grown tired of constantly having to look at what she considered to be both an eyesore as well as a persistent and embarrassing reminder of their good money gone to bad. When we arrived, she made it abundantly clear that we were always her choice for installing their patio, but her husband was being "cheap" and had gone with some "jack leg" instead. Unsurprisingly, though, Mr. Jack Leg landscape contractor had seemingly vanished into the ether without a trace and could not be found.

The installer they hired ultimately deceived and took advantage of them. Consequently, the couple's dismay and disappointment weighed heavily on them, a constant worry creating a great deal of tension and leaving the beautiful relationship we witnessed when we first met them practically in unrecognizable shambles. They could not avoid the backyard catastrophe their patio project became, and facing it daily took a deep emotional toll, such that they seemed unable to move beyond it.

She completely blamed her husband for their predicament; however, she could not have been more critical of him than he was of himself. He blamed himself for all that had transpired, for not seeing it coming, for allowing them to be duped, and for letting her down. His shame and her fractured trust were the manifestation of the hidden emotional cost of falling victim to dishonest business practices.

This problem could only be repaired by taking the pavers up, removing the sand, installing a proper base, and then rebuilding the patio. Now, in addition to the money this couple had shelled out to Mr. Jack Leg to do the job incorrectly, they now also had to bear the cost of removing the faulty work and reinstalling the patio properly. So, in actuality, to save a few dollars they paid twice for this project. You simply cannot measure or estimate the cost of the time lost, the emotional strain placed on their marriage, or the resulting stress caused by the entire episode.

Over the years, my husband's *pay me now or pay me later* viewpoint has proven true on an unfortunate number of occasions. It is truly bittersweet because although it is important for us to make money as a business, there is never any celebrating acquiring a client when you are called in after lawns (or lives) have been destroyed at the hands of the unethical or the inexperienced. The only satisfaction and reward comes in the end as you see the look of contentment and relief when projects and outlooks appear much better and brighter than before we arrived.

"I've been blessed to find people who are smarter than I am, and they help me to execute the vision I have."
—Russell Simmons

So, what have you learned thus far?

Now, armed with a little more knowledge under your belt, we certainly hope you can appreciate that when selecting a landscape professional, there are a number of elements worth taking into account above and beyond merely a difference in price. All landscapers, goods, and services are not created equal. If having the job done correctly the first time and getting the best value for your money are important to you, then you cannot go wrong employing an honest, properly licensed landscaper with experience (or if not licensed one with the practical hands-on industry expertise necessary to complete your project). Never overlook a solid reputation, a properly trained staff, the right tools and equipment, and the required insurance even if that landscape professional charges a bit more.

An honest landscaper will not engage in the pricing game. He or she knows that doing so does both parties a grave disservice because invariably somewhere along the way, they will be forced to cut corners and compromise the integrity of your project to get the job done at the agreed upon price. An honest contractor is not ashamed to make a profit on a fair and ethical bid, can properly establish and defend the value associated with her price, and will not cut price just to secure the work. If you really want to work with the guy who shows up and asks if he can borrow your pick, your shovel and a pair of work gloves, you have my word I will not try to stop you. However, I honestly believe you are much too smart not to want your contractor to at least make a profit on your job. Profitability helps ensure that the contractor will be around in the future should you have a warranty issue, need additional quality work done, or even to answer your question of, "Can you tell the name of that beautiful tree with the dark red leaves you planted behind the mailbox?"

CHAPTER 2

EXPERIENCE ALWAYS ENHANCES THE EXPERIENCE:

Don't Underestimate the Skill Your Project Requires

"Experience keeps a dear school, but fools will learn in no other."—Benjamin Franklin

Please trust me when I tell you that at no other time in history has the damage and destruction caused by unskilled landscapers been more widespread. The relative ease of entry into the industry means that with a minimal investment almost anyone can start a landscaping business. I personally consider this a positive aspect and a great opportunity for those possessing an entrepreneurial spirit and wish to enter the industry and grow a successful business based on quality work, ethical practices, and valuable service to customers.

Still, over the past seven years or so, a surge of untrained, unskilled, "fly-by-night" landscapers, with absolutely no intention of learning the craft or increasing their knowledge of the industry have capitalized on the ease of entry to fly under the radar and make a "quick buck" wherever, whenever, and however they can. When the recession hit and North Carolina's jobless rate soared, it seemed that anyone with access to a lawnmower and a leaf blower hit the streets as a landscaper without having taken the time to acquire any education, training, or experience.

Even worse, these self-appointed "contractors" are not licensed or insured and, therefore, are not accountable to anyone. As such, a number of unreliable, unskilled, uninsured, and unscrupulous operators not only wreaked havoc on property owners' landscaping and property, but also their wallets and their faith in the industry. Additionally, those who have been duped by these imposters always seem to speak of them in terms of a common character trait which they all invariably appeared to possess. Almost without fail, their victims say of them, "He or she seemed like such a nice person." Until the mess hit the fan, that is.

Listen, do not be sucked in by nice! Nice is for neighbors, customer service reps, and your sister's boyfriend who is coming over for dinner to meet the family. Nice is not a factor sufficient enough to expose your wallet, your property, or your peace of mind to the real risks that exist. Nice cannot substitute for experience. Many licensed, skilled, experienced landscape contractors are undercut in bidding wars by those who lack the knowledge, experience, and/or the intent to properly perform the quality of work for which they are hired. They perfect the ability to appear nice—big smile, warm greeting, firm handshake, empathy, and all, to camouflage what they lack in aptitude and ethics.

Adding to the problem is the whole reality television, do-it-yourself phenomenon. Every week popular shows like *Desperate Landscapes, Yard Crashers,* and *Turf Wars* flood the airwaves and American living rooms, prompting many to march bravely onto the do-it-yourself battlefield, and fail miserably. While these shows are often interesting, educational, and highly entertaining, they should come with a warning statement: "Caution! The do-it-yourself projects on screen may appear easier than they actually are!"

Being addicted to Home and Garden Television (HGTV) and the DIY Network myself, I know these shows can be highly inspiring and leave property owners reeling and giddy with tons of creative ideas. On the other hand, as an industry person, I also know they can be somewhat misleading, sometimes to the point of being downright deceiving. With time-lapse video and a little creative editing, what comes across as simple on television can leave unwitting homeowners full of false impressions and unrealistic expectations.

It is all too easy to underestimate the level of skill required for the actual landscape or hardscape installation when watching these shows. After all, as viewers we all hear the charge to invite a few friends over and knock this project out in a weekend, right? While some homeowners definitely possess the required industrial skills, hand tool savvy, green thumb, and patience to get the job done, others might be better served and avoid the learning curve, potential do-overs, and a multitude of costly mistakes by hiring a licensed landscape contractor for the job.

As a homeowner, it can be difficult to discern whether or not the landscape professional you are hiring has all the right qualifications. However, an influx of untrained professionals and an increase in unresolved complaints demands you to step up your game and do your due diligence. Not every landscaper is a licensed contractor, and homeowners often do not know the difference between a landscaper who holds a licensed contractor designation, and one who does not, and who is required for which job.

I also want to make it clear that not every unlicensed landscaper is ill-equipped to perform a task, has intentions of ripping you off, or is trying to make easy money by cheating you or the system. Likewise, licensing is not necessarily a measure of competence or integrity. At a minimum, however, licensing does at least suggest a certain degree of professionalism and commitment, which puts the odds on your side. The best practice is to always minimize your risk by making sure the company you are considering has the three R's of good business: reputation, responsibility and reliability. This is where doing a little investigative homework on the front end, can save you a great deal of time, money, and frustration on the back end.

Experience matters, and I highly recommend you not only check references, but if possible, look at past examples of work the contractor has completed that are similar to your project, just to make sure the quality meets your expectations. Trust the saying, "Talk is cheap," as many a contractor or company over exaggerates their knowledge, skill, and expertise just to land the job and subsequently, proves unable to produce a satisfactory finished product.

When evaluating potential contractors, do yourself a favor and avoid the trappings of the verbal promise, a broad, warm smile, and a firm handshake. Make them put their money where their mouth is and prove to you that they bring experience similar to the size and scope of your project. Otherwise, how can you be certain they possess the competence and aptitude to accomplish the work?

CHAPTER 3

DO SWEAT THE SMALL STUFF:

No Maintenance, No Warranty, No Insurance – No Deal!

*"Physically you are a human being, but mentally
you are incomplete.
Given that we have this physical human form,
we must safeguard our mental capacity for judgment."*
—Dalai Lama

Look for the maintenance and warranty clause in your written agreement.

Maintenance and warranty agreements are not just limited to automobiles and appliances. The day your landscape project is complete (the wedding day) is always exciting, the finished product gives every appearance (the wedding pictures) of a project well-done, and the next few weeks of backyard barbecues to show off your new outdoor living space (the honeymoon) are loads of fun, but the future of your landscape project (the marriage) is what is most important.

Despite following proper planting procedures, and providing sufficient aftercare, there will always be instances where plants simply do not survive the process of being transplanted. Plants are living things, and just like us, can suffer great trauma when uprooted from one home and moved to another. The landscape professional you hire should warranty their workmanship and plant materials for a specified amount of time, usually about one year, to give the plants time to go through one growth season, and replace any plants that fail to survive, at no charge. Make sure the terms of the warranty, any exclusions, as well as any care instructions for the plants they have installed on your property, are clearly expressed in writing.

Both at the beginning of your project and once the project is complete, you should be clear on the who, what, and where of your plant materials:

- *Who* cares for the plants?
- *What* care do the plants require?
- *What* happens if my plants do not survive?
- *Where* can I find that written on my agreement?

Some landscape companies also perform maintenance and may include a maintenance period in their agreement. Some property owners feel confident enough in their ability to take over the maintenance themselves, but even in this instance, they need to be aware of how this affects the warranty.

A warranty can give you the confidence and reassurance that the contractor believes in and is willing to stand behind his or her work. In fact, I would be leery of proceeding with any contractors unwilling to voluntarily warranty their work. After all, if a company does not have any faith in its workmanship or the quality of materials it will bring to your project, then why in the world would you?

Don't skimp on insurance!

It surprises me just how often homeowners fail to confirm whether a company has formed a legal business structure, let alone holds a current certificate of insurance, until after something has happened; at which point it is often too late.

Though the appeal of doing business with the uninsured (and unlicensed) contractor as opposed to hiring a credentialed contractor who actually believes it is important to pay for insurance may be the "perceived" cost savings, in reality, uninsured contractors expose you to significant financial risks, up to and including the loss of your home. Take a moment, and think about it! If a contractor does not carry or discontinued insurance to save on premium costs, they likely have no way of repaying you for any damages caused to your property—like cutting down a tree that crashes through your house—and certainly no way of taking care of an employee who might be hurt while working on your property.

Should a claim arise, what initially appeared to be a money-saving decision could result in a huge rate increase, or even worse, complete denial of the claim or total cancellation of your homeowner's policy for knowingly hiring an uninsured contractor. Consider the financial devastation to you as the property owner, in the way of medical expenses and lost wages, should this contractor's employee sustain personal injury while working on your property.

As a property owner, it is your responsibility to protect yourself. Before a contractor does any work at your home, verify that they possess both a license and insurance. Do not take for granted that he or she has insurance simply on the virtue of any claims made on an impressive looking company website, premium business cards, or glossy full-color promotional flyers. Confirm for yourself with your local licensing board, and ask for current proof of both General Liability Insurance and Workers' Compensation Insurance to be submitted before any work commences.

Generally speaking, in North Carolina most one-person operations are exempt from carrying Workers' Compensation Insurance. In fact, the state only requires businesses that regularly employ three or more employees to carry the coverage; however, this exemption does not apply to General Liability Insurance. The contractor's General Liability Insurance will make you whole for the damage caused by the tree that was once growing too close to your house, but due to contractor error is now inside your house, while the contractor's Workers' Compensation Insurance will cover any employee should the employee be injured while on the job.

"Genius is the talent for seeing things straight." —Maude Adams

I certainly hope my message is becoming clearer to you now. I see too many instances in which the person who is being entrusted to help plan your outdoor space, incorporate your vision, and protect your property and your best interests is not selected on the basis of skill or knowledge about plant material, irrigation, soil compaction or drainage, or possessing the proper license, permits and insurance, but solely on a price that seems too good to be true and very often, is.

If you believe installing a proper landscape is as simple as digging a few holes and dropping some plants in the ground, then I would say, "By all means, go for it!," but the truth is that it is simply not that simple. What often seems like an inexpensive deal at first usually ends up costing more in the end, with the property owner left holding the bag. I witness this in both landscape and hardscape construction, such as retaining walls, decks, and concrete paver installation. Someone is always in trouble when I see unqualified contractors advertising prices well below the cost of what a legitimate installer can reasonably do the job for, not to mention make a fair profit, enabling them to stay in business.

CHAPTER 4

BUT WHAT DOES IT ALL MEAN:

A Landscaper by Any Other Name

"It's not titles that honor men, but men that honor titles."
—Niccolo Machiavelli

In this industry, titles vary considerably and are loosely used by anyone who professes to be a "landscaper" or do "landscaping". You may also hear the industry itself referred to by a variety of titles, like: green industry, landscape industry, lawn care industry, and the like. In addition, I have on many occasions been asked to explain the differences among a landscape architect, landscape designer, landscape contractor, landscaper, and a lawn professional, as well as the differences between a landscaping company and lawn care company and the services each type of company provides. Truly, there are some notable differences.

Many people outside the industry incorrectly believe the titles all refer to the same general services and segments of the industry, partly because their use is very relaxed.

Industry people do not really do much to lessen the confusion because when asked they often find it easier or more convenient to say, "I'm a landscaper," or "I own a landscaping business." The titles however, may entail many different functions depending on what part of the country you are in and whether the individual holding the title has a license, certification, or other credentials stating he or she is, in fact, recognized as a professional in their specialized area of landscaping. Although a lot of people and companies offer multiple services, there are major significant differences, ranging from educational requirements, training, ability, and the services one is legally permitted to offer.

One major industry-wide ethical concern involves individuals or companies who present themselves as something they are not in order to secure a job. When a consumer seeks to secure a contractor for a landscape project, it is not uncommon for most people to mistakenly expect that individual or company to be a one-stop shop, cable of doing it all.

To increase your knowledge of their respective functions, let's take the time to define each one:
Landscaper: This is probably the most commonly used title, and typically everyone in this industry is considered to be, in one way or another, a landscaper. A landscaper operates in both interior and exterior spaces, increasing the aesthetic appeal of both by planting flowers, trees and shrubs. A landscaper may also provide overall care and maintenance of the lawn or landscape, including mowing, trimming, seeding, fertilizing, mulching and weed control. Although in most cases, landscapers require no formal

training and are not licensed or regulated these individuals can and do become highly skilled through practical field experience and voluntary participation in optional classes and certifications.

People often refer to the individual solely responsible for their lawn maintenance (mowing, edging and trimming), or landscape maintenance (maintaining the health and appearance of existing trees, plants and shrubs), as their landscaper. Because services differ, putting a few definitions in place will enable you to better understand service offerings, including what each service may or may not include, as well as service limitations.

Landscaping: Full service and comprehensive, landscaping is the art of improving the aesthetic appearance of an area of land through the design and installation of not only plants but other landscape features such as lighting, water systems, patios, walkways, decks, and retaining walls. In the state of North Carolina, when the cost of a landscaping project exceeds thirty thousand dollars a North Carolina Landscape Contractors' License is required.

Lawn Care: Lawn care specifically covers the care and treatment of grass in a lawn. Most lawn care programs include seeding, fertilizing and aerating, as well as weed and insect control.

Lawn Maintenance: Lawn maintenance or yard maintenance, as it is sometimes referred to, are services that concentrate strictly on the lawn's turf areas and is usually limited to mowing, trimming and edging.

Landscape Maintenance: Landscape maintenance is the practice of keeping existing plants, trees, shrubs and grounds in a clean, healthy, safe and attractive state. Services may include the planting of annuals, weeding, fertilizing, pruning, landscape lighting, snow removal and other projects as required for enhancing and maintaining lawns, gardens and grounds.

Landscape Architects (LA): This landscape professional focuses on the planning, design, and direction of spaces in order to make them beautiful as well as functional. Individuals in this field determine the overall big picture, giving more consideration to objects in a space and how these objects work together and in harmony with the natural environment. LA's plan and design land areas for projects such as golf courses, parks and other recreational facilities, hospitals and school campuses, airports and highways, industrial and commercial properties, as well as residential sites. There may be little knowledge of construction, installation, plant materials and environmental factors beyond their scope of expertise.

Landscape Architecture is a specialized field that requires licensing. To obtain a license to practice in North Carolina, the N.C. Board of Landscape Architects ("National Examination," n.d.) requires applicants to have a four-year degree in landscape architecture, a minimum of four years practical experience under the supervision of a licensed landscape architect, and a passing score on the Landscape Architect Registration Examination (L.A.R.E.).

Landscape Designer: While a landscape architect requires education and licensing it is very common to see individuals performing many of the same duties as a landscape architect, without the degree or licensing. These individuals are known as landscape designers and this is probably who most residential property owners with small scale projects will want to work with. Like the landscape architect, the landscape designer plans, designs and beautifies a space, but due to lack of licensure will be limited in the size and scope of work they can undertake.

While formal licensing and training is not required, these individuals often have a very strong background in horticulture and pay close attention to environmental factors and proper plant selection. A landscape designer may provide conceptual and planting plans to a homeowner but may not offer architectural design services, including: construction plans, landscape construction details, irrigation plans, grading and drainage plans, nor may they submit required drawings to homeowner's associations or city, state, or county governments.

Landscape Contractor: This is the individual or team who is responsible for your physical installation and executes the plan for lawns, plants and hardscaping that have been drawn up by a landscape architect or designer. After installation they can maintain the landscape, control pests and weeds, and keep the outdoor space looking its best.

Landscape contractors are commonly referred to as landscapers because it is said that they physically scape the land. They possess the experience, knowledge, and skill to build structures; install trees and plants; prepare estimates and contracts; repair and maintain gardens, lawns, shrubs, vines, trees or other decorative vegetation; install and maintain drainage systems and water features; and construct fountains, pavilions, retaining walls, fences or walks, arbors, patios, driveways, green roof systems, rain water harvesting systems or cisterns.

A licensed landscape contractor is knowledgeable about weather and climate conditions, soil conditions, what materials work best together, which plants grow well together, plant growth habits, and what should be planted where for maximum sun, shade or space to meet required growing conditions.

❧

It is worth noting that not every state requires licensing for landscape contractors, and among those that do, regulations vary. In the state of Florida, for example, the landscaping industry is not regulated. A Florida landscape contractor need only obtain a federal tax identification number and register their business with the state to operate. The only Florida landscaping businesses regulated by the state government are those offering landscape architecture services.

The state of Oregon, on the other hand, requires a landscape contractor to obtain two licenses ("Steps to Becoming Licensed," n.d.), the individual landscape construction professional license along with the landscape contracting business license. In the state of North Carolina, landscape contractors are regulated by title 89D, *The Landscape Contractors Law*, which exists to safeguard life, health, and property and maintain a high professional standard in the industry. The law makes it illegal for any person or entity to use the landscape contractor designation without first making application, fulfilling the formal education or minimum experience requirements, passing a written examination, and being licensed by the North Carolina Landscape Contractors' Licensing Board.

The relationship between a landscape contractor and a landscape architect is a very important one, and the roles of both are critical to a successful landscape. Even the most experienced landscape contractor will have trouble executing a bad plan. Likewise, the best landscape architect can deliver a great plan, but in the hands of an unskilled landscape contractor, the execution of the plan will more than likely be subpar.

As you can now see, there is a vast difference among the varied roles and functions of a landscape architect, a landscape designer and a landscape contractor, and those engaged in the business of yard yardwork. While the term landscaper is often utilized broadly and loosely as a catchall, it is not. Many who identify themselves as a landscaper have no special training, licensing, skill, or experience beyond mowing lawns, trimming hedges, or arranging a few flowers in a garden; however, there are those who conceal that fact if offered a greater opportunity for a larger scope of work, even if it is outside of their expertise.

Just because your neighbor's lawn care person does an exceptional job of mowing lawns, and you really liked the spring begonias he or she planted in your neighbor's window boxes, that does not necessarily mean this is the right individual for your backyard renovation project. Here are a few questions to ask your prospective landscaper or landscape contractor:

- *How long have you been in the business?* If an individual landscaper or landscape contractor has been in business for a while, chances are that business will still be doing business should you need its services again. You furthermore need to know whether or not that landscaper or landscaping company has been in business under the same name. Multiple name changes can spell big trouble.

- *What operating or professional licenses do you hold?* I simply cannot put enough emphasis on the importance of contractor credentials. Does the landscaper or company have a business license? What certifications, licenses, or practical experience do they have? Does he or she carry General Liability Insurance and, where required, Workers' Compensation Insurance?

If you choose to work with a contractor who does not have the proper credentials in place, beware that you do so at your own peril.

- *Tell me about any project like mine you already completed?* Unless you just like being a Guinea pig, look for a landscaper or landscaping company that has a successful completion history of projects similar to yours. Twelve years in business as a landscape maintenance company does not necessarily equate to their possessing the knowledge and experience necessary to successfully complete your particular landscape installation project. In order to ensure he or she possesses the competence to meet your specific goal, insist on seeing evidence demonstrating successful experience on projects similar to yours.

- *How are you personally involved in my project?* Do not assume that the person you have been speaking with and to whom you have communicated the vision for your project is the person who will actually be working to implement your project. In fact, you may or may not see this person ever again. In many cases there will be a supervisor or a crew leader who is in charge of the project and can answer your questions. If this is the case, you may want the comfort of knowing the person you originally connected with will check in periodically to ensure that quality standards are being met and work is progressing as planned. Clarify this up front so that you might lessen the chance of any surprises being sprung on you later.

- *Will subcontractors or your own employees complete my project?* Let's say, for example, your project includes some new landscape planting, walkway pavers, and an irrigation system. If your landscape contractor is not licensed to install irrigation systems, then the right, legal, and ethical thing for him or her to do is subcontract that portion of the work out. Nothing suspicious there. It would be a huge red flag, however, for your landscape contractor not to use their own personnel to install your plants, trees, and shrubs. Even though your landscape contractor is responsible for hiring any necessary subcontractors, you should insist that all subcontractors are held to the same credentialing standards as your contractor.

When subcontractors are used, I highly recommend for homeowners to protect themselves with a very simple document called a Subcontractor Lien Waiver. The lien waiver basically states that the contractor you hire will make all payments to subcontractors or to anyone who supplies goods and materials for your project. This simple document guarantees that you will not be held responsible and the subcontractor cannot place a mechanics lien for their services on your property if the obligation is not met. This can be a separate document, or it can be a clause in the contract; however, since the laws governing subcontractor liens can vary from state to state, it is important that you educate yourself on their use, validity, and enforcement in the region where you live.

- *Can you provide a reference list of past clients?* References are a great place to start, but they will not be of much value to you if you do not ask the right questions. It is of the utmost importance to get feedback from the most non-biased sources you can. This means you will want to eliminate the favorite aunt who thinks her landscaper nephew hung the moon, the girlfriend or boyfriend who just adores everything their *Sweet Cheeks, Baby Cakes* or *Pooh* does, and the best buddy who would say anything to help out a friend. Ask the contractor specifically if any of the references provided are family members or close friends. If you do not ask, this fact will likely not be divulged. In addition, make sure you get references for recent work, as well as work that is a little older, four to seven years perhaps. It is easy for a job to look good when it is first finished, but what you want to know is how the work has stood the test of time.

Also, get a range of references that reflect the various communities in which your contractor provides services. Is he or she giving consistent good results in every neighborhood, or can you detect a pattern in which certain neighborhoods are serviced more expertly than others? Finally, since we all have different needs and expectations, it is not enough to simply ask a reference, "So, what did you think about landscaper Bob?" If you really want the "dirt," pun intended, on your landscape contractor and really get a good feel for whether this is the right contractor for you, you will need to ask questions that specifically address areas of importance to you.

You need answers to questions similar to the following: Was he or she punctual? Did he or she communicate with you throughout the project? Did you feel like you had a good understanding of the process? How would you describe working with his or her crew? Did you experience any delays or budget issues? Were you pleased with the results? Would you use their services again?

The answers to the following questions will give you a much clearer picture of the individual or company you are planning to hire.

- *Will I receive a written estimate?* A good written estimate should include important details such as the scope of work that is to be performed, who will perform the work, an approximate timeframe for project completion, payment terms, and terms of warranty. When executed by both parties, this becomes your contract. Do NOT proceed without one!

- *What is included in your services?* You do not want to find out after the fact that things like cleanup, debris removal, and disposal is your responsibility. If your project requires a permit from your local building department or code enforcement agency, is the contractor able to get that? You should not be responsible for these things.

- *How much time will it take to complete my project?* This will depend on the size and scope of your project, but your contractors should be able to provide you with a fairly accurate timeline estimate that takes into account normal weather conditions as well as unexpected events. Get it in writing so you know what to expect. Not only does this help you have an idea of when your job will be finished but it also gives you a schedule to hold your contractor accountable to.

- *Once my project is underway, what is the procedure in case of cost changes?* Since final project costs can vary from the original estimate or price quoted, it is a good idea to agree up front and in writing just how these changes will be handled. Material prices can increase from the original quote, and issues can arise during your project that escalate your cost without your knowledge or consent. A clause in the contract that addresses how unexpected costs over and above the budgeted amounts are to be handled keeps you in control and on top of your project budget.

- *Do you foresee any issues with the project? Are there any special concerns that I should be mindful of?* In the process of visiting your property, taking measurements and assessing the area for the work to be done, it is possible for the contractor to spot something of potential concern. He or she may make a mental note of it but may not say anything to you about it unless it becomes an actual problem. This is not necessarily an attempt to deceive you in any way, but more of an individual working style. Some people are reactive, while others are proactive. I was reactive, but thanks to my wife, I now prefer to address potential concerns on the front end, so they are less of a problem, or not a problem at all, on the back end. This is also what I recommend for you. While a reactive contractor may believe there is no need to mention something that or may not be a problem, he or she is very likely to disclose the potential issue if you ask up front. The way I see it, the fewer surprises, the better.

For those of you who reside in the state of North Carolina, below are sections of the Landscape Contractor Licensing Statutes which will provide you with important information you need to know when someone presents him or herself to you as a landscape contractor. For those outside of North Carolina, please check the corresponding statutes along with the licensing, registration, or certifying board in your state. A full version of the statutes can be located easily by doing a quick, internet search.

"§ 89D-11. Definitions. (N.C.G.S § 89D-11-3-4)

(3) Landscape contractor. – Any person who, for compensation or other consideration, does any of the following:

1. Engages in the business requiring the art, experience, ability, knowledge, science, and skill to prepare contracts and bid for the performance of landscape services, including installing, planting, repairing, and managing gardens, lawns, shrubs, vines, trees, or other decorative vegetation, including the finish grading and preparation of plots and areas of land for decorative utilitarian treatment and arrangement.

2. Practices the act of horticulture consultation or planting design for employment purposes.

3. Constructs, installs, or maintains landscape drainage systems and cisterns; provided the landscaping contractor makes no connection to pipes, fixtures, apparatus, or appurtenances installed upon the premises, or in a building, to supply water thereto or convey sewage or other waste therefrom as defined in G.S. 87-21.

4. Designs, installs, or maintains low-voltage landscape lighting systems, provided (i) the work does not exceed the scope of the exception set forth in G.S. 87-43.1(7) and (ii) the low-voltage lighting systems do not exceed 50 volts and constitute a Class II or Class III cord and plug connected power system.

5. Engages in the construction of garden pools, retaining walls, walks, patios, or other decorative landscape features.

(4) Person. – An individual, firm, partnership, association, corporation, or other legal entity.

"§ 89D-12. License required; use of seal; posting license. (N.C.G.S § 89D-12A)

(a) Except as otherwise provided in this Chapter, no person shall engage in the practice of landscape construction or contracting, use the designation "landscape contractor," or advertise using any title or description that implies licensure as a landscape contractor unless the person is licensed as a landscape contractor as provided by this Chapter. All landscape construction or contracting performed by a partnership, association, corporation, firm, or other group shall be performed under an individual who is readily available to exercise supervision over the landscape construction and contracting work and who is licensed by the Board under this Chapter.

If you have a legitimate complaint regarding work performed by any landscape contractor licensed by the state of North Carolina, the N.C. Landscape Contractors' Licensing Board can help you with that complaint. When the board receives notice of your complaint, which must be in writing, it will advise the contractor of the details of your grievance. The contractor then has thirty days to submit a written response to the board. If you have, however, engaged the services of a contractor not licensed by the N.C. Landscape Contractors' Licensing Board, and during the course of your project he or she violates a number of safety laws, fails to adhere to your contract, has poor workmanship and issues they refuse to fix, or just disappears in the middle of your project and will not return your calls, you forfeit that layer of consumer protection. As an unlicensed contractor, this individual is not held to the standards of the state's licensing board, and the board's authority to aid you does not extend to your use of non-licensed individuals.

CHAPTER 5

HELP! THERE'S A LADY ON THE LAWN!:

A Tale of the Unskilled Applicator, the Weed Killer and the Crime Scene

"The right tool in the wrong hands, or the wrong tool in the right hands, will always end up withdismal results."
—Daniel Stoelb

Lillie McBloom was excitedly making preparations for her club's annual Ladies on the Lawn event. She was honored to have been selected to host the group's annual fundraising social this year and Lillie aimed to achieve perfection; every single detail would be an illustration of sheer flawlessness. With the cellist lined up, the caterer chosen, and the ideal seasonal menu selected, Lillie was now deciding on just the right centerpieces and table accents to add a sophisticated garden feel to the event.

She was certain that the large ornamental trees and stunning hydrangea gardens her expansive backyard offered would make a beautiful backdrop for the affair. It was an elegant looking outdoor space, thanks to her late husband who had the gift of a green thumb and very much enjoyed working in the yard. However, a close inspection would reveal the presence of a handful of trespassers poking about in her lawn, a few random patches of forever pervasive and always invasive dandelion weeds.

Most of the time, the presence of the bright yellow blossoms did not bother her much. Mrs. McBloom took pride in her nicely manicured lawn but was not obsessively bothered by less than perfect grass and could certainly tolerate a few springtime dandelions. Yet this was different. Her good friend, fellow club member, and social arch nemesis Mrs. Bea Hive was last year's Ladies on the Lawn hostess, and boy, had Bea set the bar high! There was no doubt about it, the party crashing dandelion weeds would have to be ousted!

Mrs. McBloom mentioned her dilemma to C. D. Guy during his weekly lawn mowing visit, and C. D. gladly quoted Mrs. McBloom a price for eliminating the weeds and assured her the lawn would be picture perfect in plenty of time for the affair. He immediately made a quick trip to the neighborhood garden center where he perused the aisles for the right product to deliver the right results, one guaranteed to annihilate those dastardly dandelions that dared to interfere with Mrs. McBloom's plans for garden party domination. Spotting a well-known brand he easily recognized, C. D. grabbed a bottle from the shelf and smiled as a quick examination of the label revealed an ever so convincing money back promise of absolute success. "Ahh," C. D. raised an eyebrow and nodded to himself, "This will definitely do the trick." Now armed with the latest, advanced, most powerful, guaranteed money back product he could find, C. D. hurried back to obliterate the dandelion threat from Mrs. McBloom's lawn.

He put on the gloves and mask he had just purchased at the store, tucked his pants inside his rubber boots, and tightened the cord on his wide brimmed hat. Looking as though he was preparing for intergalactic travel, C. D. paused for a moment, with fists on his hips, to enjoy the beautiful spring breeze blowing his way. He smiled in satisfaction with the task he was about to perform and hoped Mrs. McBloom would be watching him work from her window.

Several days later, with a refreshing mint julep in hand, Mrs. McBloom headed towards a reclining lawn chair to enjoy an afternoon read. She sat down and allowed her gaze to sweep across her yard, soaking in all of all the beauty, color and comfort it provided, while simultaneously making a few mental notes for what was soon to be the most fabulous party of the season. Then, without any warning at all, her mind spun uncontrollably as it suddenly began to process the images her eyes had taken in, and she abruptly and unexpectedly realized that something was terribly amiss. What manner of catastrophe had befallen her beautiful lawn?!

A horrified Mrs. McBloom dropped her mint julep, raised both hands to her face, and belted out a chilling, anguish-filled scream. What was once a lush, beautiful yard, tastefully adorned with colorful trees and blooming flowers, now looked like a horticultural crime scene! Patches of dying, brown grass covered the once thriving, green lawn. Sickly yellow blooms drooped sadly from wilted hydrangeas, and the leaves on her beautiful eastern redbud tree were twisted and curled with its once bright, magenta, pink flowers now severely and pitifully discolored. Poor Mrs. McBloom clutched her pearls with one hand, held her wig in place with the other and fainted right there on the spot.

Weed killers don't destroy; unskilled applicators do.

A pesticide is a biological agent that deters, incapacitates, kills, or otherwise discourages pests, including but not limited to insects, disease, and weeds that destroy property or cause a nuisance. The application of pesticides is considered an especially dangerous or, in legal terms, an "ultra-hazardous" activity. In all fifty-one states, the Environmental Protection Agency (EPA) requires pesticide applicators be certified as competent, and to undergo recertification every three to five years. Although certification programs are conducted on the state level, there are strict federal standards these programs must also meet. These federal standards and mandatory certification requirements are meant to ensure that pesticide applicators are knowledgeable and have an understanding of pesticide product labels, along with the established methods of proper pesticide application. Furthermore, strict adherence to these requirements and standards practically guarantees safe, effective pesticide use, thereby reducing the risks to human health and the environment, including wildlife, endangered species, and groundwater.

Even among properly trained, certified, and the most careful of applicators, weed killer error or other damage can still easily occur, whether the wrong chemical or too strong of a chemical is used, or someone simply fails to thoroughly clean remaining pesticide out of a sprayer before using it to spray fertilizer. So understandably, for the untrained applicator, mistakes and the resulting consequences can often be worse. A few notable incidents of both skilled and unskilled applicator error have occurred in recent years:

In 2012, Rob Olson, a property owner in Minnesota, accidentally killed 40,000 square feet of his lawn after applying a product he thought would only kill his weeds. According to the story reported by Boyd Huppert, KARE-11 in Minnesota (Huppert, 2012), Olson discussed the product with three employees at the garden center where he purchased five bottles, and everyone assured him that he was purchasing weed killer. However, a product use booklet attached to the bottle did explain that the product was not for use on grass or any other "desirable" garden plants. A supplemental warning printed on the bottle similarly advised that in addition to killing grass, the product would also prevent reseeding from occurring for up to as much as six months. Mr. Olson believes product packaging is to blame and hopes someone at the company will make this right for him.

This next story of an Ohio university forced to replace almost all of its grass is even more recent:

In May of 2014, staff writer Max Filby of the *Courier* (Filby, 2014) reported that the University of Findlay was being forced to replace approximately three quarters of their lawn after an unnamed lawn care company accidentally applied weed killer instead of fertilizer to the grass. It was an unfortunate mistake that affected fifty-four acres of a campus that works hard to maintain its appearance. It was estimated that replacing the grass could cost as much as 2.1 million dollars, largely due to the amount of labor required to reseed or re-sod that much land.

Ironically, as I was working on this project, word of a similar incident killing two-thirds of a high school football field arrived in my email inbox:

According to the Chicago Tribune (Chamberlain, 2015) on September 4, 2015 the lawn care company responsible for maintaining the St. Edwards Central Catholic High School football field inadvertently applied weed killer instead of fertilizer to the teams' playing field. The mishap, which occurred when someone grabbed the wrong bottle of chemical, ultimately destroyed more than 65 percent of the stadium's turf. The school considered the incident an honest mistake and the lawn care company, who was not named in the report, was working diligently to correct the problem. The St. Edwards football team was forced to give up its home field advantage for four of their five remaining home games.

The EPA takes pesticide application very seriously and property owners should as well. Weed killers are designed to kill invasive, unwanted plants. Unfortunately, it is all too easy for weed killers to damage or even kill wanted plants if proper care is not taken. Mistakes and the outcomes of improper application can vary greatly. Some chemical errors will have minor consequences, which can be repaired quickly and inexpensively, while other fixes will come at a great financial cost. Some problems appear immediately, while others take time, even up to the following season, before symptoms appear. Often, a great number of errors generate only inconvenient, aesthetic implications. Still others will pose a threat to children, pets, produce, and drinking water.

In the case of our poor Mrs. McBloom, to address her dandelion issue, C. D. Guy headed to the local home improvement store and purchased a well-recognized, national brand of weed killer. Assuming he knew exactly what to do, he returned to the McBloom home and proceeded to "spot spray" everywhere he found dandelion weeds. After all, to C. D. Guy this appears to be exactly how they do it in the product's commercials. What C. D. did not know is that the product he had chosen is a non-selective herbicide formulated to kill every green thing it touches.

Furthermore, in addition to accidentally taking out some patches of grass along with the dandelion weeds, unbeknownst to C. D. the spring breeze he enjoyed that day had caused the spray to drift into the hydrangea garden as well as onto a beautiful and very meaningful ornamental tree; the eastern redbud which was the last thing Mr. McBloom had planted before his passing.

Fortunately, the damage to the tree was minimal with only the flowers being affected, and the eastern redbud, though sickly in appearance at present, will make a full recovery. If a stronger chemical had been used, the soil could have been damaged extensively; making it extremely difficult to grow new grass. Under the circumstances, however, Mrs. McBloom's lawn can be reestablished, the dying hydrangeas can be replanted, and the garden will be as lush and lovely as it always has been. But not a single one of these miracles will happen in time for the annual Ladies on the Lawn affair.

Some of the most common causes of weed killer or herbicide damage include the following:

- *Spray Drift.* When spray vapour, droplets or dust particles become airborne and move away from the target area what you have is a condition known as pesticide spray drift, or more commonly drift or overspray. This drifting spray is potentially harmful to nearby plants, as well as neighbouring properties, and can expose people, wildlife and the environment to harmful pesticide residue, so be careful. Since windy, warm or sunny conditions can increase spray drift damage, it is best to spray herbicides when the weather is calm and, whenever possible, cloudy.

- *Container Contamination.* Any residue that is left behind in a contaminated watering can or an unrinsed or poorly rinsed sprayer can inadvertently expose your wanted plants to weed killer.

- *Leaching.* Excessive watering or rainfall following a herbicide application can cause residual weed killers to leach into nearby plant beds.

- *Absorption.* When the application rate is exceeded or in areas where light, sandy soil allows weed killer to penetrate deeper, underlying plant roots may absorb residual herbicides.

- *Contaminated Mulch or Compost.* While mulching grass clippings back into the lawn can prove beneficial, it is important not to mulch with recently treated mowing clippings or use compost that may retain any active herbicide.

- *Vandalism.* Yes, as difficult as it may be to believe, there are some dirty, rotten scoundrels out there who wage full scale herbicide warfare by way of deliberate lawn or plant vandalism. These pests, sometime jealous or nasty-for-no-reason neighbors, deliberately spray your trees and plants; kill your grass, and even wrongfully clear and cut things from your property.

Based on their degree of toxicity, the EPA has classified pesticides as either general use, those available for use by the general public, or restricted use, those pesticides which are not available for use to the general public. The EPA determined that when applied in accordance with their directions for use, general use pesticides will typically not cause unreasonable adverse effects to people, pets, wildlife, or the environment. However, the EPA also determined that restricted use pesticides have higher risks and probabilities of causing unreasonable adverse effects on humans and the environment, even when applied in accordance with their directions for use. Therefore, restricted use pesticides must only be sold to and applied by a certified pesticide applicator, or under the direct supervision of a certified pesticide applicator. North Carolina requires both landscape contractors and homeowners who apply restricted use pesticide to be certified pesticide applicators. There are strict penalties for both selling restricted-use pesticides to an unlicensed applicator, as well as applying restricted use pesticides without a pesticide applicator license.

The story you are about to read is true. The names have been changed to protect the innocent and the inexperienced.

I have maintained the properties of a handful of residents in a community of homes for about seven to eight years now. Over these seven or eight years, the gentleman occupying the corner property at the entrance of the community has undoubtedly grown accustomed to seeing me come and go. He is an elder gentleman, retired, and keeps a keen eye out for everything happening in the neighborhood. Sort of like a one man neighborhood watch. For the purposes of this anecdote, we will call him Dr. Homeowner (aka Doc). Although I do not maintain Doc's property, he and I are quite friendly. I always take the time to wave or speak as I enter or exit the community, or occasionally stop to enjoy a brief chat, time permitting.

He has a very nice row of mature Leyland cypresses planted at the rear of his property. You probably know the Leyland well. It is a fast growing evergreen that can grow up 100 feet tall and takes on a pyramid like shape, wider at the base and pointy at the tip. According to the National Christmas Tree Association, in the Southeast, Leyland's are the most popular choice for Christmas trees, but their fast thick growth, along with the fact that they have foliage year round, also makes the Leyland cypress a very popular choice for barrier planting. I guarantee you have noticed them growing, several in a row, providing a nice screen between neighboring properties. Since Doc's home is at the entrance of the subdivision, the trees afford him the perfect amount of privacy from the main road.

One day as I was leaving, I noticed some damage to the foliage of the tree on the end. Something appeared to be eating away at the lush green leaves, leaving the appearance of brown bare spots in their place. The culprit in this case was not hard to spot—big, bad, ravenous bagworms! These bagworms made their home in the tree, and a feast of the free abundant food it provided. It appeared to be an early stage problem, localized to a small area of just the one tree; however, if left unchecked, not only would the infestation spread throughout this tree, but the wind could easily transport larva down the line and cause significant damage or even kill the entire row of trees. There was simply no choice. The squatting bagworms would have to be evicted.

On my next visit, I caught Doc sitting on his porch. We waved to each other as usual, and he quickly jumped to his feet and walked in my direction. As I began to slow my truck and roll down the window, I was not sure if Doc was aware of the bagworm problem, but I definitely wanted to bring it to his attention. Midway through our chat, I pointed towards the rear of his property and said, "I've noticed you've got a little damage to one of your trees back there. Has your lawn guy (we will call him Guy Landscapes, or G. L. for short) mentioned anything about bagworms to you?" Looking back towards the trees Doc squinted thoughtfully for a second and scratched the back of his head before answering. "No, I don't recall him saying anything about it." So, I suggested Doc mention it to G. L. on his next visit, and Doc assured me he would. I considered it done and did not think much more about it.

The following season, somewhere around late summer, I noticed the damage to Doc's Leyland spread to an even larger area of the tree. This could only mean one thing – the bagworm eggs had survived the winter, hatched in the spring, and had since been feeding on the leaves. I was quite surprised to not only see the problem still existed, but had now become an even larger problem, and wondered if perhaps Doc had forgotten to mention it to G. L. Even if he did forget, if I could see the damage from the street in my truck, surely the lawn guy could see it riding right past it on a mower! Not wanting to overstep any boundaries, I belabored over whether or not to say anything. But as a lover of all things green and growing, I would never have forgiven myself if I remained quiet.

A couple of visits passed before I would catch Doc outside again. When at last I did, I stopped, we talked a bit, and I finally got around to commenting on the growing damage to the tree and asking Doc if he had remembered to mention the bagworms to G. L. last year. "I sure did," he answered, "And I thank you again for telling me about that too." Then Doc continued, "He took care of it for me right away." "He did?" I asked, completely failing in my effort to not sound overly incredulous. "Yeah," Doc answered, "I believe he said he sprayed it with something. You're talking about my peach tree, right?"

His answer floored me. Even from my sitting position, I could feel my knees buckle. The peach tree!

A large peach tree, healthy, fruit bearing, and free of any disease or insect infestation, grew on Doc's side lawn. The only thing I ever observed in this beautiful tree was a squirrel or two, enjoying the free, fresh fruit buffet.

Of all the tree and shrub pests, bagworms are among the most easily recognized because as the name implies, bagworms reside in a bag, a visible cocoon made of worm silk and plant debris that is attached to and hangs downward from the trees branches, much like a pine cone. I have often heard people refer to the look of bagworms as "hanging like a tree ornament." The worm constructs this bag as its home and lives inside very contently and comfortably, oblivious to anything going on in the outside world. It only has to stick its head out to eat. When the infestation is small, as was the case when I originally spotted it and pointed it out to Doc, the most effective way to get rid of them during this stage is to simply pick them from the tree and destroy them. As long as the problem is small and insignificant, not only is picking the cocoons from the tree effective, but it is also an inexpensive method of control. And this was certainly a problem that started out small and insignificant, but then something went terribly, terribly wrong.

Now, in the movies this is the point where, in order to help fill in that essential backstory leading up to the main sequence of events, they would interject a flashback scene. Well stay with me for a moment as we hold things here, and roll back the tape to the previous summer...

When I mentioned the bagworm problem to Doc, I pointed in the direction of the Leyland cypresses planted along the boundary line at the rear of his property. However, I had not taken into consideration that the unknowing property owner might innocently and mistakenly think I was referring to the peach tree planted on the side lawn, several hundred feet ahead of the Leyland's.

I can only imagine Doc's conversation with his lawn guy going a little something like this:

"Listen, the other gentleman who does a few of the yards out here—you know him, that real nice, good-looking fellow that stops and talks sometimes? Well, he said it looks like some kind of worm is eating at my peach tree back there. "

Then, Guy Landscapes, not having any knowledge of pests in the landscape and depending completely on Dr. Homeowner's interpretation of the information, picked up a bottle of who-knows-what from who-knows-where and sprayed the peach tree for a problem it did not have. Yes, bagworms can and do attack fruit trees, but that was not the case with Doc's healthy peach tree.

Feeling somewhat guilty, I wanted to take the blame for not communicating it more clearly, but in reality, this was not a communication error. It was not Doc's fault, nor was it mine. Someone qualified in the area of pest identification and pest management would only have had to take one look in the direction of those trees to know Doc Homeowner mistakenly interpreted my message. However, knowing that *something* had been brought to the homeowner's attention would serve as enough information for the experienced individual to quickly identify the location of the problem, the nature of the problem, and how to treat the problem. It is important to understand the expertise and the qualifications, along with the limitations, of your lawn care professional.

If you experience a situation that warrants weed, pest, or insect control, the experienced staff at your local agricultural extension agency can often easily identify the invader for you. In most cases, all the staff needs is for you to provide a clear picture of it. Once they identify it, they can also recommend the best treatment options.

Remember that even as a private property owner, you have a responsibility to protect yourself, others, and the environment. It is important that prior to using any pesticides yourself, you read label directions carefully and follow those directions closely. If you believe you may need a professional pesticide applicator, take the time to get a feel for the skill, competence, and experience of the person or company you will be hiring. Here are a few questions you will want potential applicators to answer:

- *Experience matters, as do licenses and insurance; do not be shy about asking!* Ask to see a copy of the applicator's pesticide license, which should be in their name, or the name of the person in their company who is responsible for supervising pesticide use.

- *Has the company been sued or fined for unlawful pesticide use or practices?* It is important to use and dispose of pesticides in a safe and ethical manner. Those who do not are accountable to the law.

- *What products will he or she use?* No one should be using their own secret family formula that saved the family farm back in 1876 and has since been passed down from generation-to-generation. It is required that all pesticides be registered with the U. S. Environmental Protection Agency.

- *Will he or she provide you a copy of the product labels?* Request a copy of the product labels so you will have a record of what was applied and when. Also, find out if what he or she plans to use is the least toxic alternative to address your specific problem. Again, even when it comes to pesticide application, be wary of the "lowest cost" trap as this may not be the best deal in the long run.

- *Are there any steps you should take to prepare or protect yourself, your family, or your pets?* Both pests and pesticides can pose a potential health hazard to you, your family, and your pets. In fact, every year hundreds of children and pets unsuspectingly fall victim to pesticides they accidentally encounter in their environment. In preparing to address your pest problem, your applicator should inform you whether you or your family should avoid treated areas for a specific period of time, if it is safe for Miss Kitty and

Duke to roam freely, or if dishes, toys, or other items should be put away or covered.

- *How will the product be applied and are there any potential adverse effects?* Sprays can remain wet for a while and be absorbed through the skin when touched. Powders and dusts can remain on plants and later be accidentally inhaled or even cling to an animal's coat, resulting in eventual absorption or even transfer into the home and subsequently to the family. Pesticides can also drift to an unsuspecting neighbor's property. Nausea, sweating, rapid heartbeat, vomiting, diarrhea, loss of appetite, muscle weakness, lethargy, and dizziness are all symptoms of pesticide poisoning. As you can see, these symptoms can be easily confused with other illnesses, like a cold or the flu.

- *How soon can you expect to see results?* This, of course, will vary by product and what specifically is being treated; however, knowing up front will help you set realistic expectations.

- *Will follow-up treatments be necessary?* Any follow-up treatment should be specific to your individual situation and not presented to you as a fixed monthly or quarterly treatment schedule.

Also, beware of companies that use pest invasions or disease as tactics to scare the business right out of you. Yes, unscrupulous lawn care companies will throw around phrases like "infestation" or "lawn disease" to get their evil grip on you and try to sell you on prevention treatments that your lawn may or may not need. Because conditions are always present and ever-changing, I do not believe we can ever fully avoid pests or disease, but we certainly should, as much as possible, try to reduce the risk of exposure. Proper and effective programs for risk reduction require the operator to gather certain information about your lawn and educate you on the presence of any pathogens should any be found. Do not let anyone sell you a blanket disease prevention program without a thorough explanation of what it entails and proof of why it is recommended treatment for your lawn.

If you follow these simple tips, I believe you can competently and confidently hire your next weed or pest control applicator.

CHAPTER 6

NAYLED TO A TREE:

*How Giving Safety the Brush Off Can Leave You
Out on a Limb*

*"People don't get injured in the tree care industry; they get
killed."*—Sam Hill of Sam Hill Tree Care, Dallas, TX

Mr. Berrie finally came to the decision to
have a large tree on his property cut down; an
old oak with several large limbs hanging danger-
ously above the house, causing Mrs. Berrie to
fret miserably. She had been on him to do something about it since last winter's ice storm resulted
in extreme damage to several of the neighbors'
homes and property. While their immediate next
door neighbor had never complained, Mrs. Berrie was also concerned that several of the tree's
branches and limbs extended past their property
line, encroaching onto his. On this particular day,
it just so happened that as Mr. Berrie was leaving

the hardware store, C. D. Guy and his long-time employee Rustie Nayles were in the parking lot drumming up business with flyers that extolled *"The best rates in town on all your landscaping and lawn care needs!"* right across the top in large, bold letters.

"Excuse me," Mr. Berrie called out, quickening his pace to catch up with the duo, "Do you gentlemen do tree work?" And before Rustie Nayles could inform Mr. Berrie otherwise, C. D. Guy rushed past him, shook Mr. Berrie's hand, and with the warm smile and charm of a *really nice person* and all the confidence and pride of an experienced tree care professional, he beamed "Best tree work in the business, sir! How may we be of service?"

Two weeks later, Rustie found himself thirty-five feet above ground with a rope tied around his waist and chainsaw in his hand, cutting limbs away from the big red oak in the Berries' yard. Rustie apparently "secured" himself to the tree with a rope and was quite pleased at the thought of his old Boy Scout knot training coming in so handy. He realized a professional tree cutter would probably wear a safety harness but knew there would be no need to ask C. D. about one, especially since they only just borrowed Mr. Berrie's chainsaw to do the cutting with.

Adrenaline coursed through his body and his pulse quickened causing Rustie to feel both nervous and excited at once. Although he had never so much as pruned a tree, let alone cut one down, he did have a little experience trimming hedges and felt pretty assured about handling a chainsaw. The high elevation made him giddy with anticipation, and he was certain that with C. D. directing him from the ground, the mighty red oak would yield to him in no time.

Rustie's confidence grew as the first few branches fell perfectly to the ground. As each branch submitted to his weapon of limb destruction, Rustie lowered himself a bit and proceeded to tackle the next. A couple of times he stopped long enough to watch the large limbs rebound. That was the biggest surprise, he thought; he had no idea the springy branches would bounce when they hit the ground.

The chainsaw whirred again and after several moments, another branch surrendered, making another clean decent to the clearing underneath. Boy, those YouTube videos had sure come in handy. Rustie felt invincible, more powerful and in control than he had ever felt before. He decided to himself that when this was over, he would ask for that raise again. He was sure this time there was no way C. D. could refuse him. But little did Rustie know, this shady tree deal was about to be cut very short, and very soon.

Rustie sawed the next branch off very close to the trunk, and under its own massive weight, the heavy branch broke free. The branch began to fall and, SMACK!, it unexpectedly crashed into another branch with an impact that caused it to detour from its straight route to the clear landing at the base of the tree! Taking a scary change of direction, the wayward limb see-sawed upward and swung terrifyingly back towards Rustie.

Rustie tried to move, but unfortunately, there was no time. The limb struck Rustie sharply and squarely, knocking him off balance. Rustie's heart seized as he felt himself falling, his arms and legs thrashing in a desperate endeavor to regain control. But his efforts proved futile and he was thrown against the tree's trunk with a startling, dull thud...

He actually welcomed the sharp pain as a signal that he was yet alive; however, everything in him hurt. The rope, once tied around his waist, now held him suspended precariously upside down by the ankle. Now dangling upside down and in pain, Rustle's morning had taken a horrific turn; confident beginnings morphed into wild-eyed disbelief, and all hopes of a raise shattered before him as he watched the rest of the scene play out.

The branch, which he had expected to fall straight to the ground, had completely veered off course. It crashed through the roof of the Berrie's house, and with another giant smack, converted the antique dining room table Mrs. Berrie inherited from her great-grandmother into a pile of splinters.

C. D. desperately wanted to take control of the calamity unfolding around him, but in his paralytic state of disbelief his mouth failed him and his body refused to move. In the meantime, however, an outraged Mr. Berrie barreled towards him, shouting expletives and waving his fist in C. D.'s direction.

Dazed and unmoving, C. D. wished the kid with the camera phone would magically disappear and wondered if this day could possibly get any worse. He had no idea just how soon he would have the answer to his question. In the aftermath of the mayhem, a faint, almost inaudible *"crack"* boomed like thunder in the distance, immediately catching everyone by surprise and putting them all on keen alert. Mr. Berrie abruptly stopped swearing, the kid aimed his camera phone back towards the tree, still dangling upside down, Rustie braced for impact and every muscle in C. D.'s body tensed in trepidation.

Seconds later it came, another crack, slightly louder than the first, immediately followed by the clamor of falling, and finally coming to an end with a raucous, sickening thud, the shattering of breaking glass, and the relentless blare of a car horn. The disturbance to the tree had caused a previously compromised limb, possibly injured during last winter's storm, to give way and collapse, coming to a halt on top of the Berries' next door neighbor's car; completely smashing the windshield, ripping through the rag top, and demolishing the driver's side window of a custom restored '55 Chevy Bel Air Convertible.

Like the Berries, a great majority of property owners will sooner or later find the need to hire a company for tree trimming or removal services. Perhaps a major storm has left damaged trees on their property, a mature tree on their property is encroaching on their neighbor's property, or a dead or diseased tree is posing a threat to life or property. If you ever find yourself in this situation, you should be wary of amateur tree cutters foraging neighborhoods with chainsaws, looking to make a quick buck. This is especially common following hurricanes and tornados, snow, ice storms or other severe storms, and heavy winds.

Tree care is an altogether different discipline. The trimming and removal of trees is arguably one of the most dangerous occupations in the U. S. and probably the most hazardous in the green industry. Every year, scores of even the most careful and skilled workers are severely injured or, even worse, killed while performing their job duties. Among the leading causes of fatalities ("Tree Trimming Safety For the Landscaping and Horticultural Services Industry," 2006/2009) are being struck or crushed by falling trees and limbs; falls from trees, lifts, rooftops and ladders; electrocution when cutting near power lines; and severe impact, such as being thrown against a tree or pinned against another structure. According to Kansas State Research and Extension, some of the most common injuries sustained in tree cutting accidents include eye injuries; scrapes and lacerations; cuts and amputations from using tools and heavy equipment such as chainsaws, hacksaws and chippers; animal and insect stings and bites; and exposure to poisonous plants (National Institute for Occupational Safety and Health, 2009).

This information of course is not intended to frighten you, but to heighten your awareness of the risk and potential for injury of which you should be keenly aware, whether attempting to tackle tree cutting and maintenance yourself or hiring it out to someone else. Tree cutting and removal is dangerous work that requires the right professional, the right equipment, and the right process. And as I mentioned in the previous section, it is important to take a step back and consider the enormous financial liability you may be forced to absorb when engaging an unskilled, uninsured tree trimmer. What would be the chances of C. D. Guy holding General Liability or Workers' Compensation Insurance, if he could not provide his own chainsaw for the job? I sure hope C. D.'s low price deal was worth the cost Mr. Berrie will now have to pay as a result of damages to his own property, his neighbor's property, along with Rustie's injuries and lost wages.

Let's close this section with a few safety precautions I feel deserve your attention:

- *Spectator Safety.* Nothing attracts onlookers, especially curious kids, like the buzz of a chainsaw and the crashing of debris. In any work zone, safety must be a top priority. Do not forget that when people visit our property, both home and business, we hold some responsibility for their welfare. In short, if someone is injured due to hazardous conditions on our property, we are responsible, and this responsibility includes medical treatment and possible compensation for lost wages and additional expenses.

  I strongly recommend that you ask anyone not directly involved with the work of taking down or trimming the tree, to vacate the area. If necessary, erect a barricade around the worksite to prevent access. Taking this precaution may sound a bit extreme, but it is better to be overly cautious than suffer the hindsight effect of woulda, coulda, shoulda.

- *DIY Safety.* To many observers and ardent do-it-yourselfers, tree work can look deceptively easy. But just because you have the time and the tools to tackle a project yourself does not necessarily mean you should. Things can and do go wrong. So, please think twice before letting your inner daredevil loose with a case of Coors at your side and your best buddy on hand to back you up.

Every headline of a homeowner who has suffered blunt force trauma from a fallen limb while trimming trees on his property leaves me utterly grief stricken. In fact, if I could pass a law barring property owners from trimming their own trees, I would do it in the blink of an eye. It would certainly save the lives of many do-it-yourselfers, as well as the lives of well-intentioned neighbors and friends who offer their help. In planning to do these jobs, the amateur tree cutter tends to focus only on the two or three limbs he or she plans to cut.

However, the experienced arborist knows that not only must the target branches be included in any plans, but the entire tree and its surroundings must be factored into the equation as well. Experienced arborists respect the fact that they are entering into a potentially perilous situation and therefore take appropriate precautions. While they do take risks, these risks are extremely calculated and in turn, call for extreme preparation, as well as the right training, the right tools, the right equipment, the right work ethic, and the right partner. Most importantly, they make it their business to understand everything about the work conditions and environment for each individual project.

In contrast, homeowners sometimes unwittingly take the most ill-advised, unnecessary risks.

One of the most unsettling scenes personally witnessed was that of a homeowner trimming limbs from a ladder propped up against a tree. This, if you have not yet guessed, is not good. Soft soil and grass does not form a stable enough foundation to support you on a ladder, especially when you are constantly climbing up and down or sawing back and forth with a sharp blade. The slightest shift or misstep could cost you big time or even be your last. If the work required cannot be reached from the ground, it is time to call in a professional.

- *Preventive Safety.* In addition to the occupational hazards and the dangers to unskilled tree cutters, trees can also pose a major threat to innocent civilians. I recently came upon my wife in quite an emotional state as she was reading the story of an infant who suffered a skull fracture and his young mother killed after a branch collapsed on them in a Georgia park. According to the report, mother and son had taken a seat on a park bench after playing on the swings. She heard the crack, grabbed her son, and attempted to flee out of harm's way. Unfortunately, she was not fast enough to avoid the falling limb and died after being crushed beneath it.

  Tragic incidents such as this occur too frequently and reading about them in the local newspaper or hearing of them from news reports or colleagues, neighbors and friends never gets easier. Incidents involving a tree or branch falling for no apparent reason, on a completely windless day, striking a vehicle that happened to be passing at the moment, or the person who happened to be sitting or lying underneath, or walking or running by, occur at schools and parks, zoos and playgrounds, on streets and highways, private business and government property, and in front and backyards across the country.

But trees do not just drop limbs for no reason. Falling limbs are usually a sign that a tree is not doing well or has suffered some type of trauma, either natural or man-made. Branches that snap during high winds or a winter freeze can hang for years before falling. Maybe you have noticed one or more hanging in your own yard or even at your place of business. Because they appear to be so high up, they seem insignificant and harmless and are easy to disregard. Tree branches however, are often heavier that we think. And from the basic laws of physics, we know an object accelerates as it falls. By the time someone realizes what is happening, he or she hardly has the chance to get out of the way.

While environmental hazards will always exist, by working together we can help reduce the risk to life by reducing vulnerabilities and threats of potential disaster looming in our surroundings. This requires policing our properties a bit more closely in order to identify, assess, and reduce any risks posed by dead, dying, dry, decayed, diseased, or damaged trees.

Whether personal property or business property, it is important to regularly assess the condition of your trees for broken, injured, or otherwise compromised limbs. Is there evidence of decay? Are any trees leaning? Is there risk of any broken, dead, or dry branches potentially falling from a tree? If you see signs of trouble, do not wait. Nothing and no one can predict when that tree or limb will finally collapse. Obviously, none of us can completely prevent these types of tragedies. But, if we each do our small part, proactively assessing and addressing the most significant risks, we can certainly mitigate the possibilities of property damage, injury, or even death.

CHAPTER 7

BREAKING STORY:

Towering Grass Lands Local Lawn Company in Hot Water

"A shady business never yields a sunny life."—B. C. Forbes

From the time he was a young boy, C. D. Guy never had any doubt that he would someday see his name in lights and his face on the screen. He knew he would make headlines but certainly never imagined it would go quite like this. It was the local 6 o'clock news, and what seemed to C. D. to be a life-sized bobble head of him was in the top left corner of his television screen. Underneath this ghastly head shot was his name, Cornelius Decker Guy, and underneath his name the subcaption read, "Landscaper Evades City; Residents in Uproar." C. D. cringed.

His favorite field correspondent, Lark Spur, was live and on the scene, narrating the rueful

story of C. D.'s evasion and dereliction of duty in
her signature reporter voice:

"At the corner of Mid-City Boulevard and
Brownsboro Street, waist high grass nearly covers a bus stop bench. At another vacant lot on
Lackey Road, the next street over, one neighbor
informs me that the grass has reached a height
of over two feet, well above the heads of many
young children. And the residents here are fed
up and fired up." The news coverage then cut
to someone the caption identified simply as,
"Ginger Orchard, Lackey Rd. Resident". Ms.
Orchard seemed a bit nervous, but her confidence seemed to grow along with her anger:

"I guarantee you it's not been cut a single time this year. It's like we're living in a
jungle. You've got 'possums, snakes and
rats—great big rats too, about the size of
cats—running through here. How am I
supposed to feel safe letting my babies
play outside? It makes the entire neighborhood look bad!"

The coverage then cut back to Lark Spur,
standing by ready to interview someone she
identified as "April Raines, Vice President of the
Purdy Neighborhood Watch Association" who
needed only minimal prompting to launch into
her own tirade:

"Some of the city-owned lots are starting to look like abandoned fields Lark,
a personal dumping ground. People are

starting to use them to discard unwanted furniture, tires, machinery—you name it. My husband walks our two dogs through the path down here, and he says there's even an old washer and dryer back in there."

Then Lark Spur reappeared on the screen to sum up the story for the viewing audience:

"And the residents and community leaders are not alone in their frustration. Bob Katz, acting Director for the Office of City Services, tells me a private lawn maintenance contractor, C. D. Guy of Shadyscapes Lawn and Landscaping, Co., was contracted to mow vacant lots starting mid-May. The company, however, is not living up to the terms of the agreement. According to Katz, Shadyscapes Lawn and Landscaping was awarded the contract after submitting the lowest bid to cut 346 properties throughout the city. So far, the company has done only about fifty.

Katz further informs me that the city simply does not have the manpower or the equipment to go out there and manage these properties, which is why the city hires this work out to a contractor every year. Furthermore, C. D. Guy has not appeared at any scheduled meetings to discuss the performance issues. Last Tuesday, the O.C.S. sent a letter to the company giving them fourteen days to perform under the contract or the contract would be terminated. In the meantime, the

O.C.S. expects another contractor to be in place at the end of the fourteen days, and are asking the residents to be patient. WICU News reached out to Shadyscapes Lawn and Landscaping for comment, but the company has not returned our calls.

This is Lark Spur, reporting from the field. Now, back to the studio."

Lark Spur then looked directly into the camera and flashed her signature smile, the smile that C. D. Guy had admired so much until this very moment.

Abandoning the contract, refusal to perform, and failing to fulfill the terms of the agreement are complaints not uncommon to the landscape industry. This is often a byproduct of irresponsible bidding, a lack of skill, shortage of labor, unsuitable equipment, scarcity of funds, or any combination thereof.

What was C. D. thinking? He knew that he did not have enough mowers, and the few he had were not nearly big enough. Not only that, his one employee was recovering from an unfortunate tree cutting accident and would not return to work for several weeks still. He had planned to hire a few people, but hardly anyone had their own transportation, and the ones who did would not work for minimum wage. C. D. was in well over his head. He was awarded the job based on his low bid, but soon realized there was no way he could complete the task. C. D. was simply incapable of meeting the City's needs.

It is common practice in both the public and private sector to use a traditional competitive bid process whereby "the lowest responsive and responsible bidder must be

chosen." Sometimes in bidding, an honest clerical error is made; numbers may have been inadvertently transposed or perhaps a line item was calculated incorrectly which results in one bidder's price being substantially off from the rest. In North Carolina, if a legitimate clerical error is found to have been made on a government contract, there is a process by which the bidder may withdraw their bid without penalty. This is a good thing. This practice ensures that one party does not get stuck with the risk of working with someone whose price is "accidentally" too low, and the other party is not trapped in a commitment they simply cannot fulfill. Unfortunately, C. D. did not make a clerical error.

There are also times when a party receiving the bids (not talking government here) thinks something may be a little "off" with the numbers, but remains silent since the potential error seems to be in his or her favor. There is a rush of excitement, and the voice of reason is drowned out by the sounds of a Vegas jackpot going off in their head. "Cha-ching! This must be my lucky day!" Or so they think.

If you have been paying attention up to this point, you know a contractor's loss in miscalculating is not necessarily your gain—that is unless you consider inferior work, delays, and major headaches to be a gain. A low bid may not be a clerical error, but more an error in judgement. There are contractors who win bids at low prices and are either very well aware, or lack the wherewithal to know, they cannot complete the job for that price. As a result, what they deliver is subpar work or the poorest performance you can imagine. In some cases, after being awarded a job, a contractor will realize his bid was not only too low to make a profit, but that moving forward with the job will actually cost him or her money. Instead of being "upside down" in the job, they choose to abandon the contract altogether.

In order to minimize overhead, a contractor who has bid too low may also deviate from the plans or specifications. Surprisingly, this is not always after realizing his bid may have been too low but is instead an intentional practice during the bidding process. In essence, this contractor has his own set of rules that he bids by. The objective is to simply win by any means necessary, and the basic guidelines do not allow for bidding the project fairly or ethically. While the other bidders are pricing the job based on exactly what is called for in the project plans and specifications, this contractor is pricing and, if awarded the job, installing materials of a smaller size, lesser quality, and reduced quantity than what is called for in the contract.

This is a process that gives the dubious bidder an unfair advantage over the ethical, by-the-book bidders. If the practice goes undetected, or even worse, ignored, unsuspecting property owners lose big time in a game they were not even aware they playing. Imagine, if you will, sitting down at a local restaurant where you have ordered and paid for the petite filet, but a big mouth burger comes to the table, your six piece shrimp cocktail arrives with only five shrimp, and oh, your throat is parched when the menu clearly states refills are free. These are concerns you would easily recognize and address immediately, right? After all, you are a highly skilled and experienced diner, eating out for as far back as you can remember. Anyone thinking of trying those shenanigans with you had better think again! But in an arena in which you are not so much the expert, your lack of experience can leave you vulnerable and exposed. Enter an opportunity for those who would seek to prey on your inexperience, and are confident that in more cases than not, you will be none the wiser to their duplicity.

Unless a property owner is themselves knowledgeable, or otherwise has engaged the services of a client representative or project consultant, not getting what you have paid for often goes unnoticed, unaddressed, and is entirely unacceptable. A project consultant serves as someone who can examine the bids to ensure they meet specification, ensure the bidder has the skill, judgement, integrity and ability to perform the contract and then follow the project to completion to ensure it is being executed according to contract specifications. This individual works exclusively on behalf of you, the property owner.

I make it a habit to maintain project plans and specs for jobs I have bid within the past three years. At times I am just curious to see how the project turned out, but every now and then, that curiosity is driven by nothing more than remaining aware of the price the awarded contractor bid for the job.

A project executed well, whether by myself or someone else, is a beautiful sight to behold. I am happy to say most contractors are remarkable; they want a satisfied customer and take a personal sense of pride in a job well done. But I can never seem to get beyond the surprise of visiting a finished project and seeing a beautiful plan carried out unacceptably. These are executed with plant sizes much smaller than identified in the contract specifications, significantly fewer plants installed than the number listed on the planting plan, trees noticeably leaning because they were not staked as called for in the specs, or dead plants which were not replaced as required by the contract warranty.

The honest, ethical, competent bidder, one who is pricing and will implement a project according to the project specifications, cannot compete with a bidder of questionable ethics and dishonest intentions. Their prices will just not align. Before you deem a price too high, take a moment to consider, "High in comparison to what?"

A low price does not always mean you have saved hundreds or, in some cases, thousands of dollars. What looks like a great estimate could cost you in time, quality, performance, and ultimately even higher costs. It is worth taking a step back from the bid and ensure you have gathered enough information (past performance, right equipment, necessary skill, sufficient staff, etc.) to safeguard the success of your project.

CHAPTER 8

ABUNDANT VINES AND
SPARSE GRASS:
Getting to the Root of Your Patchy Lawn

*"No customer walks into your business, gives you money and
then says, 'Dissatisfy me, please.'* —Bill Quiseng

Two years have passed by since Rose Thorne
hired C. D. Guy to manage the grounds for Abundant Vines Missionary Church. When C. D. Guy
began managing the property, the church was
relatively new; built less than five years prior. It
was an attractive site, but the members thought
the bare, patchy spots throughout the lawn, where
no grass would grow, greatly detracted from the
church ground's overall curb appeal. Since the
lawn had been seeded when the church was built,
church members were mystified as to why the
grounds looked so sparse.

Rose hired C. D. soon after finding out many of her church members used his services and after noticing his flyer for lawn care services on the church bulletin board. Rose scheduled a meeting with C. D. who really impressed her as a nice, likeable guy. In fact, she discovered C. D. was the cousin of Abundant Vines' choir director, and her very good friend, sister Tee Leaves.

Nonetheless, church members pointed out many concerns, and the church trustees were anxious to get to the root of why two years after hiring C. D., the property looked no better than it did prior to contracting him. In fact, some areas looked worse. Upon reviewing their documents to verify the services they should be receiving, Rose realized C. D. never gave the church a written contract. However, in studying the invoices, Rose discovered that in addition to billing for monthly grounds maintenance—mowing, edging, weed eating, and trash removal—C. D. also invoiced the church for putting down lime, fertilizer, and grass seeds in both the spring and fall of each year.

What's more, the church operates a weekday childcare facility. On several occasions the childcare staff had reported that C. D.'s employee has a nasty habit of dropping his cigarette butts around the playground area, an obviously inappropriate, disgusting and hazardous thing to litter a children's play area with. Still, after addressing this concern with C. D. on multiple occasions, the problem persisted.

Rose knew it was past time that the church terminated its relationship with C. D. It was only in the church's best interest to hire someone who ran a more professional service and could actually improve the look of their lawn. Rose was reluctant however, as she tried hard to live by the "good book," and simply did not want to hurt anyone's feelings. Besides, not only did C. D. come highly recommended by several of Abundant Vines' members, but it turns out he is also the relative of the pastor's third cousin twice removed and another of Rose's dear friends; sister Ruby Spice. This made Rose extremely anxious and very concerned about how firing C. D. might be received by her friends and congregation.

No one likes the feeling of paying for something he or she is not getting, and no one should be forced to. Feeling vulnerable and as if you are being strung along is even worse. Being trapped in a deal gone bad, or any arrangement that is not working for you can be stressful and disheartening. An arrangement which is clearly not in your best interest, or in which you feel disregarded, disrespected, or taken advantage of should be evaluated for termination immediately.

I believe the majority of contractors really want to do a good job. They want to treat you fairly and, in return, just want to be treated fairly. But let's face it; even the most experienced landscaper is not perfect. Mistakes happen and from time to time, Murphy's Law is bound to rear its ugly head, and what can go wrong, will go wrong. But as

Donald Porter, a former V.P. of British Airways once said, "Clients don't expect you to be perfect. They do expect you to fix things when they go wrong."

What interests me though, is the extreme high level of tolerance we seem to have for persistent poor service. When things are about as bad as they can possibly be, we turn to a neighbor, a relative, two co-workers, and Facebook, and ask whether they think it is time for us to fire our contractor. When promises are made but not kept, calls are not being returned, no shows and late arrivals have become the norm, costs are escalating for ambiguous reasons, lawns are in shambles, and walkways are destroyed, the perpetrator is often inexplicably rewarded with one more chance.

Certainly it is not my intent to offend my female readers (although my wife assures me that I will not), but all too often women, in particular, struggle to speak up in these situations. In my humble opinion, this reluctance persists due to their fear of being rude or a desire not to hurt the individual's feelings. Please allow this tip to take root: *If* the other party held the same regard for you, this situation would likely not exist in the first place. Think about it.

"It is impossible to have a healthy and sound society without a proper respect for the soil." —Peter Maurin

Albeit for very different reasons, both commercial and residential property owners care about the appearance of their lawns. The commercial property owner understandably wants a property to exude a professional, well-groomed appearance to clients and visitors alike. The residential

property owner has an emotional and financial investment and a personal sense of pride in his or her property.

In either case, the quality of your lawn is directly related to the steps taken to establish it. Unfortunately, a very important, but often overlooked, first step in the process is an assessment of the condition of the soil in which the lawn is to be established. I am constantly blown away at the number of landscapers who consistently fail their clients, both commercial and residential, in their neglect to utilize this valuable, easy, and inexpensive tool. Countless epic lawn fails are perpetrated at the hands of landscape professionals who took the shortcut and nonchalantly disregarded the simple soil sample test.

In the countless contests for bragging rights being waged in American neighborhoods across the country no one criterion is more prevalent than the appearance of the residents' yards. Neighbors compare lawns more than they compare square footage, automobiles, or perhaps, even kids. Those vying for bragging rights, or at least a conversation worthy yard, invest immeasurable time, effort, and money into achieving lawn perfection.

In return for their investment, the property owner enjoys a number of perks, including envious stares from neighbors, compliments from friends, home energy savings, increased property value, and most importantly, an enormous sense of chest swelling pride. Hands down, the least popular neighbor is the one who seems not to care about their lawn. He or she is seen as an outcast amongst neighbors, deemed more of a nuisance than the noisy neighbor and the nosey neighbor combined. While a well-maintained lawn boosts value and pride, an unsightly yard can be a constant eyesore. It detracts from the overall appearance of a neighborhood and lowers the values of the neighboring homes and properties.

For those with a vested interest in keeping their lawns beautiful and healthy, there can be a tendency to look at the lush green carpet of grass surrounding a neighbor's home and approach it much like a science project. They believe if the neighbor would describe the exact steps taken down to the tiniest detail, and they repeat the neighbor's process step-by-step, they will inevitably enjoy the same results. If only it were that simple!

The problem is that in just about every neighborhood across the U.S., soil quality will vary greatly from house to house, and, believe it or not, sometimes even within the same yard. While some homeowners are blessed with the perfect soil for growing grass, many others must put in a little extra work in order to achieve great grass. The good news is, the perfect lawn is achievable.

Wherever you plan to establish a lawn or renovate an existing lawn area, begin with a soil analysis. Any landscaper or turf professional you hire to improve the appearance of your lawn who proceeds without the benefit of a soil analysis is wasting your time and your money. In fact, you will likely get the same results if you walk around your property, throw money around the yard, and wait for the grass to grow. In both scenarios, you lose time, effort, and hard earned cash. These are wasted trying to improve an inferior lawn without the benefit of the most critical element—insight as to how to achieve optimal growing conditions and determine the best course of action for your specific lawn.

Don't Guess — TEST!

Whenever I come upon a case such as the one with C. D. Guy and Abundant Vines Missionary, the starting point is always a simple one. Without a little assistance, the soil of many properties will lack the structure and nutrition that grass requires to grow. A soil analysis is the only means of accurately assessing what amendments a lawn requires. The test will measure the nutrients that are currently available in the soil so you can take advantage of these, as well as recommend corrective actions for any fertilizer deficiencies and pH adjustments.

Because proper pH is one of the most important soil properties affecting the availability of nutrients, lawn care professionals, as well as homeowners who care for their own lawns, often mistakenly believe lime applications (which raise pH) provide the foundation or fix-all of growing great grass. I see lawn services that go out to a property twice a year, apply lime and fertilizer, and then bill the client. If this description applies to your lawn care service, he or she is doing both you and your lawn a huge disservice.

Think of it this way. Would you give a dose of penicillin to a child who is not sick? Of course you would not! There could be many harmful repercussions. Over applying nutrients that your lawn does not need not only wastes your money, but it also creates unhealthy imbalances in your soil, which can pose harmful effects on the environment. Conversely, not applying enough fertilizer means your soil will not contain the elements essential to plant nutrition. In both cases, an environment is established in which it will be difficult for grass to grow and thrive.

It is also important to note that while the process of collecting soil samples is simple and the cost of having your soil tested is fairly inexpensive, understanding the results may prove challenging. Soil testing labs report results using turf industry terminology, often without explanation of what any of it means. Parts of it can seem completely foreign to the homeowner or landscape professional unfamiliar with soil science or chemical elements. The soil test report is undoubtedly an invaluable tool but of very little value in the hands of those unable to interpret the terms and numbers used. This may very well be one of the reasons that many landscapers forego the testing.

Nonetheless, what a soil needs cannot be determined by look, smell, taste, or feel. The only way to determine how much fertilizer and lime are required for turf establishment is by implementing a soil test. Do not let your landscaper's lack of knowledge cost you time, money, and a great deal more.

If you are establishing a new lawn or suffered disappointment at a patchy, hard-to-grow lawn where only the weeds seem to thrive, creating healthy soil is key. Work with a knowledgeable landscape professional who can establish a comprehensive plan for your lawn based on the results of a comprehensive soil analysis. The analysis will determine the characteristics of your soil, compared to the requirements of the grass or other plants you wish to grow.

Some of the changes may be: to raise or lower the soils pH, or evaluate other nutrients like nitrogen, phosphorous, or potassium that may be inadequate or excessive. Be patient and understand that while some changes may appear quickly, others may take a few years as you see the nutrient and macronutrient levels gradually adjust to the corrected ranges. Your local county extension office is also an excellent resource and will happily to provide you with a soil test kit and/or instructions for submitting a sample.

CHAPTER 9

CONCLUDING WORDS—MYTHS, LIES, AND DEMISE:

Demystifying the Contractor-Client Relationship

"There is one and only one social responsibility of business— to use its resources and engage its activities designed to increase its profits so long at it stays within the rules of the game, which is to say, engages in open and free competition without deception or fraud." —Milton Friedman

Before we part, I want to address a few commonly held beliefs that could jeopardize your search for the right contractor if you persist in holding tenaciously to them. These are myths or preconceptions possessing no basis in fact that I run into online, hear at trade meetings, and encounter in conversations with potential clients. Since the best customer is an educated customer, I decided to close by separating belief from reality and examining a few misconceptions potential clients often seem to believe are true. A couple of points will be new, but most will reiterate what you have already learned thus far; potentially in a different way.

Understandably, selecting contractors for projects around your home or at your place of business can seem a little daunting, but it does not have to be. First and foremost, contractors are no different than you. Although when selecting a contractor, ostensibly you are scrutinizing us, it is important to realize we are scrutinizing you as well. I attended a trade meeting recently where the topic of customer acquisition came up, and every contractor at the table agreed that at some point in their business they each made the decision to become more selective about the clients they take on. "All money is not good money!," declared one of the attendees and the rest of the table laughed and echoed their agreement. Are you the customer we want? Because just like you are looking for the best contractor, we want the best customers, those who understand and appreciate the value of their landscape relative to the overall value of their home and property, those who know their options and can make informed decisions. It is really no different than choosing your dentist, family physician, or pet sitter. Doing a little research and separating the facts from the opinions will make the process a great deal easier with satisfactory results in the end.

Let us clear the air by addressing some myths and beliefs so you have a better understanding regarding your dealings with contractors:

Everything is negotiable, including contractor quotes. Many people seeking the services of a contractor are under the impression that whatever price a contractor quotes is negotiable. This is just not true! Due to our lagging economy, I know many of my fellow landscape contractors are working very hard to offer their clientele and prospective clientele the best price possible while remaining competitive. I repeatedly observe firsthand the hard work these professionals put into reducing their overhead costs. Most are going to give you their very best rate upfront and not deal with the negotiation game. And as a client, I want my contractors to make a profit! Let's face it. If a business cannot make a profit, they are either not going to be around for very long or cut corners in their workmanship to make up the difference. Neither of these is a very good option.

There are actually some advantages to a business that has been and will be around. What about that warranty you have for the work they have done? How about wanting additional work done by this same contractor? This is not going to happen if the business folds. Each and every time, I will intentionally put my money on a profitable business with a staff of experienced, knowledgeable people to deliver the very best results.

How dare they ask me for a deposit. That is the most unprofessional thing I have ever heard of! Try to put your entrepreneur hat on for just a moment and understand that one of the most difficult challenges any business owner has to face is maintaining positive cash flow. The trees, shrubs, mulch, and that fancy stone you selected for your project cost a lot; perhaps a whole lot!

A contractor is not a financial institution. It is a mistake to believe he or she is responsible for funding your project. A deposit or retainer simply means you are sharing in the funding. And why not? After all, it is your project. And in most cases, the deposit is still smaller than the amount the contractor is putting into your project to get it off the ground. If you believe the deposit is too high, ask the contractor if a large deposit can be broken down into smaller draws as the work progresses.

That means there is a percentage you are responsible for paying at the completion of each stage, and this solution may be an option for larger projects that are expected to take a month or more to complete. If you do have this type of arrangement, it is important to make all payments when due. Otherwise your project may come to a complete standstill until the finished phases are all paid up.

Now, what you do not want to do is pay a deposit without having a written contract. As my wife says, "The contract is queen." There is a show I find pretty interesting that airs on CNBC titled *The Profit*. The premise of The Profit is that this wealthy entrepreneur, Marcus Lemonis, travels the country putting up his own money to help save failing businesses. He pays off their debt, throws in some working capital, invests in equipment and upgrades, and then, for a time, takes control of the company long enough to steer it back on track. He and the owner[s] then become partners.

My brain is stunned every time I see Marcus enter into a six-figure deal with people he has recently met on nothing more than a handshake. Interestingly enough, the majority of these deals end well for him. I also viewed a couple of episodes wherein Marcus' new partners reneged on the deal after spending his money. Even so, it remains a risk worthy system for Marcus. You, however, are not Marcus. You should not do deals on a handshake.

Quite honestly, having a deposit agreement along with a detailed contract is good business and just plain old common sense. It protects both sides. Contractors do not want to get shortchanged on a job any more than you do. You must feel comfortable with the contractor you wish to work with. Examine what might really be holding you back from making that deposit. Is the real issue one of trust? Is your inner voice is sending out warnings? Trust your instincts. Your feeling of unease may be a sign that C. D. Guy is not the right contractor for you. Heed the signals and find someone else.

Do not waste money on unnecessary permits. Your dream deck is at last finished, complete with custom benches and planters, an outdoor kitchen, plenty of space for entertaining, and beautiful ambient lighting to set the mood. It is absolute deck perfection. And certainly the very last thing you want to do is have that beautiful new dream deck added onto your home, just to find out you have to tear it all down. However, if you make improvements to your property without obtaining the required permits, this is exactly the risk you take. Not only that, you could be forced to remove it as well as face some hefty fines and penalties.

Permits are not mere formalities. Permits are not requests. Permits are the law! The law is there to protect you, the property owner, by making sure your project meets certain safety standards, thereby reducing the likelihood of injury to yourself or others as well as ensuring your project is code compliant. This protects your property value, makes sure you have an accurate property description recorded should you ever decide to sell the home, and since many property insurers will not cover damages caused by work done without a permit, having one, while it may seem costly or inconvenient, could actually save you money in the long run.

Contractors who try to cut corners on permits can be very convincing, giving you any number of tried and true lines: "It's not really necessary for this job." "I personally guarantee the work will be done to code." "We build these all the time without them." And the old tried and true favorite, "Trust me." DO NOT believe one word of it.

If a contractor tries to tell you that a permit is not required, do yourself a favor and pick up the phone, contact your city or state building or permit office, and verify it for yourself. Every project will not require a permit, but if you tell them what you are doing on your property, whether digging a hole to China or adding a second story addition, building code officials will gladly tell you whether you need a permit or not. Then, if a permit is required, your contractor must get one before any work ever begins. Remember, pulling the permit is their responsibility, not yours.

Word-of-mouth is the best way to go. I always felt the best compliment I can get from a customer is their repeat business or word-of mouth referral. Referrals are the secret to success for many businesses and work beautifully as long as they are utilized appropriately. However, the client's needs and the referred contractor's skill must be compatible.

I would never want a client who was happy with my backyard redesign and installation to offer me as a reference to a neighbor looking to have his or her roof replaced. Contrary to popular belief, landscape professionals do not know everything about the exterior workings of your home. While you will find many handyman services who offer everything from general lawn care and power washing, to crown molding and new tile installation, licensed landscape contractors are "generally" not exterior home improvement pros. We do not necessarily have the expertise to meet all of your exterior home care needs.

That being said, when getting referrals, make sure the contractor you are being referred to possesses the necessary skills, abilities and experience to successfully complete a project comparable in scope and size to your specific project. Successful landscapers do not perform work outside the scope of their mastery, just as your podiatrist would not be comfortable performing your root canal, your barber would perhaps balk at performing your colonoscopy, or your computer tech support would hesitate at giving you tax advice. Get the picture?

You are not purchasing a one-size-fits-all. You are looking for an experienced contractor who possesses the requisite knowledge, experience, and expertise to successfully complete your project to your satisfaction. If you are having a stone retaining wall built, you want to be referred to contractors who are experienced in masonry work, not some guy who simply mows lawns. Now, that guy mowing lawns might actually have some masonry experience and started a landscaping business that includes retaining walls, outdoor fireplaces and patios, and other masonry work, so ask questions and find out first.

If you want a specific job performed, always ask the contractor whether he or she has ever done that type of project before. An honest, responsible contractor will tell you upfront when you ask him or her to do something he or she is not proficient at and will likely provide a great referral for you. Never rely on someone else's satisfaction in a contractor's service unless you know for sure you are comparing apples to apples.

Negative online reviews are an automatic deal breaker. Online reference sources such as Yelp, Google+ and the Better Business Bureau can be helpful tools in your search for the right contractor however, since internet rants can be completely valid, blown way out of proportion, or fall anywhere on a continuum between, coming across the occasional negative online review is not necessarily cause to write off a potential contractor.

No business should be expected to have a perfect rating every time and anyone in business long enough should anticipate the occasional negative feedback. At times, cranky customers will bash a business online simply because something did not go their way and at other times, cranky customers will flood the web or social media with negative comments because the contractor truly messed up. What you want to focus on instead is the contractor's response to the situation. Were they professional or did they resort to trying to disparage the client? Was there a good faith effort to fix the problem or did they make excuses and try to explain it away?

The true professional is one who takes ownership of their work and is more concerned about making things right, than proving they are right. If they responded in a constructive and helpful way, took the right steps to fix what was wrong or went the extra mile to make the customer happy, this is a great indication of the contractor's commitment to quality service and client satisfaction and how you can expect them to deal with you.

Never trust a contractor who uses a post office box for their business. The first time I heard this one I was absolutely shocked. To this day, I am still not sure what it has to do with anything. Some contractors work out of a home office, and some work out of an outside office. In either case, there are many reasons why a contractor would choose to use a post office box on their business cards, website, or other marketing materials. In fact, I have used one for twenty years!

First, a post office box offers greater security than a mailbox, so naturally, a contractor would prefer to receive payments at a post office box. Next, anyone who has ever started a business knows that once you are open for business, your junk mail increases tenfold. If your mail is delivered to a post office box, it is easy to discard or recycle what you do not want right on the spot. And last, but perhaps of most importance, if you do business from a home office, you would not want your home address publicized on any letterhead, marketing material, or your website.

Contractors are people with families just like you. The last thing they want is someone showing up at their home unannounced, uninvited, unexpected, and unwelcome to discuss business. Not only does it cross the line of good business practices, but it is also disrespectful. Do not let a faulty assumption cloud your good judgement and keep you from making a sound, sensible decision. A contractor's choice to use a post office box has nothing to do with his or her skill, ability, or professionalism, nor is it a red flag that he or she has something unethical to hide.

The newer the trucks the more professional the company. Wrong again. A not-so-new and shiny truck could be the sign of a pennywise contractor keeping overhead down. If a contractor has a dependable workhorse that gets great gas mileage, why should he or she replace it simply for appearance sake? After all, landscaping is not clean work. Most contractors I know use their trucks mainly to haul equipment, materials and supplies for the job site. It does not matter what they drive as long as they can count on it to do the job, and you can count on them to do the job.

Conversely, it is also fair to note that a shiny new truck does not necessarily mean a contractor is overpriced. You should never presume the ability, success, or the fee scale of a contractor simply by what she drives. The vehicle is simply a means of moving what needs to be moved from one place to another.

Contractors are nothing more than scammers, con artists, and thieves. Okay, I cannot deny that horrible contractors exist. After all, dishonest, unethical, irresponsible contractors provided the impetus to write this book. We hear about them on the news, through word-of-mouth, and even catch them on video. They make fools of themselves and create distrust throughout the entire industry. But believe it or not, this represents a small percentage of contractors.

The majority of contractors are hardworking people, men and women raising their families, volunteering in the community, excited for the opportunity to make a living and a difference. They take enormous pride in their work and businesses and have great deal riding on the quality of work they produce. They want their customers to come back time after time, and they want their customers to refer them to family and friends; something that likely will not occur without some hard, honest work and use of the most skillful team of people at their disposal.

Also understand contractors are running businesses, not charities. When a legitimate contractor is establishing pricing, there are a number of expenses to consider. Some are very obvious to you, like the cost of skilled labor, quality materials, as well as the fuel and equipment needed to do your job. Though perhaps less obvious to you are other costs that must be factored in. These include rent, insurance, equipment and vehicle maintenance, office supplies, utilities, and the like.

Whether you are buying groceries or clothing, getting an oil change or a haircut, all businesses maintain operating expenses that are reflected in the cost of the goods and services you buy. It is no different for contractors. Most of the contractors I know and have the pleasure of working with work hard to keep prices fixed for as long as possible. But the responsible contractor also understands that not pricing projects appropriately could result in a struggle to make payroll, pay vendors and suppliers, or stay in business altogether. Hopefully, you can understand that too.

If you have a landscape project on the horizon, I trust I have given you some new perspectives here that have raised your awareness, challenged your preconceptions, and helped you gain a better understanding of the role both professional and consumer accountability play in achieving optimal results.

Now you should be prepared to make an informed, educated choice. Take your time, consider your options intelligently, compare bids astutely, and select a skilled craftsperson with whom you are comfortable and are confident can get the job done. Stay focused on your end-game, which is a space you will love and will give you beauty, comfort and enjoyment for many years to come. Most importantly, have fun and savor the journey. In the end, I believe you will be thrilled with your project and your landscape contractor, and probably start your own word-of-mouth referral.

ACKNOWLEDGMENTS

As we commemorate our 20th year, we realize this milestone was made possible by so many who have supported us over the past two decades.

To start, we would like to express our sincere thanks and appreciation to our clients and customers for the confidence you place in us to provide the level of service you need and deserve, and for trusting us with your colleagues and friends by way of your generous referrals. Your business, loyalty and support has allowed us to enjoy some exciting and rewarding years, weather some difficult years and emerge as a strong, highly competitive and well-respected organization.

Not only are our clients and customers integral to our success, but as we celebrate this 20th anniversary, we are grateful and well aware this milestone would not be possible without the support of our family, friends and loved ones. Your belief has sustained us and we could not ask for anything more. Thank you for all you do to contribute to our success.

To our subcontractors, vendors and suppliers – and to all of our employees, past and present, for working so hard to help us honor our commitment to provide our clients and customers with the very best at all times – we thank you!

We also extend a very special thank you to the wonderful team of proofreaders, editors, graphic designers and illustrators who were so instrumental in bringing this book to life. Working with you was a pleasure and we hope you are as happy with the finished product as we are.

The past twenty years has been a remarkable journey of exploration, discovery, faith, and amazement. We are grateful for every moment of simply doing what we love to do, for the lifelong connections we have built, and for the differences, large and small, we have been fortunate to make. As we look ahead to the next twenty years, we thank God for the incredible opportunities and for being the head of our lives and our business. We anticipate with GREAT expectation the new levels of success, reward and prosperity already prepared for us.

Thank you all, so very much; and as God has showered His blessings on us and our organization, we pray that likewise He will shower His blessing on your lives and your endeavors.

RESOURCES

North Carolina Landscape Contractors' Licensing Board: If you believe you've been the victim of unfair treatment or unethical conduct by a North Carolina Licensed Landscape Contractor, you have the right to file a complaint. Information on filing a complaint as well as the complaint processing procedure is available at the NC Landscape Contractors' Licensing Board website (http://NCLCLB.com). Select "File a Complaint" under the Laws and Enforcement tab. You may also visit the Licensees tab to find a licensed landscape contractor or verify a contractor's license.

Should you believe that you have been exposed to pesticide spray drift and have health-related questions, you should contact your physician, local poison control center, or health department for assistance. You can also contact the National Pesticides Telecommunications Network (see below for specifics).

This is also a good opportunity to verify that you have phone numbers for emergency medical assistance and for your state and county agencies.

North Carolina Department of Agriculture and Consumer Services, Structural Pest Control & Pesticides Division: If you suspect that there has been an occurrence of illegal spraying or believe you have suffered property damage due to pesticide spray drift, you should contact your state or tribal pesticide regulatory agency. In North

Carolina, your first contact should be the North Carolina Department of Agriculture and Consumer Services, Structural Pest Control & Pesticides Division who enforces pesticide laws and regulations locally. A Pesticide Specialist can be reached at (919)733-3556.

North Carolina Department of Agriculture & Consumer Services: If you are looking for a licensed pesticide applicator, each states licensing agency maintains its own database. This information is typically available to you online and you can either search for a licensed applicator or verify an applicators license. In North Carolina, a licensee search can be conducted at the North Carolina Department of Agriculture & Consumer Services website http://www.ncagr.gov/aspzine/str-pest/pesticides/data/advsearch.asp.

United States Environmental Protection Agency (EPA) Office of Pesticide Programs: For general information on the United States Environmental Protection Agency (EPA) pesticide program, call the Office of Pesticide Programs at (703) 305-5017, or visit the EPA pesticide website at www.epa.gov/pesticides/.

National Pesticide Telecommunications Network (NPTN): For information on pesticides and pesticide exposure, contact the National Pesticide Telecommunications Network (NPTN) between 6:30 a.m. and 4:30 p.m. (Pacific Time), seven days a week, at 1-800-858-7378 (toll-free) or through their website (http://npic.orst.edu/). NPTN provides pesticide information to any caller in the United States, Puerto Rico, or the Virgin Islands.

REFERENCES

National Examination (n.d.). The North Carolina Board of Landscape Architects. Retrieved from http://www.ncbola.org/exam.lasso?-session=LASession:DVrCC3ViilioSQ3aO0VTCh2UNXVn2DDC39BECF

Steps to Becoming Licensed. (n.d.). Landscape Contractor's Board. Retrieved from http://www.oregon.gov/LCB/Pages/steps_to_license.aspx

Huppert, B. (2012, July 9). Backyard Fundraiser Cancelled After Lawn Mistakenly Killed. KARE 11. Retrieved from http://www.kare11.com/story/news/local/2013/11/26/3739759/

Filby, M. (2014, May 16). Oops! Mistake Kills Most Grass at University of Findlay Campus. *The Courier, Findlay-Handcock County-Northwestern Ohio*. Retrieved from http://thecourier.com/local-news/2014/05/16/oops-mistake-kills-most-grass-at-university-of-findlay-campus/

Chamberlain, G. (2015, September 17). St. Edwards Decides to Hit the Road, Let Grass Grow on Football Field. *Elgin Courier-News*. Retrieved from http://www.chicagotribune.com/suburbs/elgin-courier-news/sports/ct-ecn-football-st-edward-field-st-0918-20150917-story.html

Ricketts, M. and Lind, S. (2009). *Tree Trimming Safety for the Horticultural Services and Landscaping Industry* (Publication No. MF2712 Rev. ed.) Retrieved from http://www.bookstore.ksre.ksu.edu/pubs/MF2712. pdf

U.S. Dept. of Health and Human Services, Centers for Disease Control and Prevention. *Work-Related Fatalities Associated with Tree Care Operations - United States, 1992-2007.* By D. N. Castillo, and C. K. Chaumont Menéndez. Washington, D.C.: Government Printing Office, 2009 (Publication No. 58(15); 389-393). Retrieved from http://www.cdc.gov/mmwr/preview/mmwrhtml/mm5815a2.htm

*"If a beautiful landscape is important to you,
then helping you achieve that goal is important to us!"*

J.W. Wright & Associates, LTD is a full service landscape contracting, management and design build firm founded in 1996 by John W. Wright, Jr., a NC Licensed Landscape Contractor and graduate of North Carolina A&T State University, with a B.S. in Landscape Architecture. Soon discovering it would require more than just a passion for landscaping to build a successful business, John invited then fiancée, Sondra, to partner with him in the endeavor. The couple married the following year; and in 2001 Sondra assumed the role of President and CEO for the corporation, taking on full responsibility for the company's operations management, while John, as Vice President, focused on his passion for project management.

Combining a 30 year background in both construction and design J.W. Wright & Associates specializes in site planning, land development, plant design, design construction, and consulting services, and provides a full range of commercial and residential landscape and hardscape services.

www.ingramcontent.com/pod-product-compliance
Lightning Source LLC
LaVergne TN
LVHW021505080426
835509LV00018B/2409

9 780983 126577